Walks in the Shropshire Hills

Area of Outstanding Natural Beauty

Walks in the **Shropshire Hills**

Area of Outstanding Natural Beauty

Dennis and Jan Kelsall

Text: Jan and Dennis Kelsall
Design: William Smuts and Lorna Jenner

Photographs: © Shutterstock, Dennis Kelsall, Lorna Jenner, Heather Price, Bob Rudham, Shropshire Hills AONB

Acknowledgements: Warm thanks to the Friends of the Shropshire Hills AONB and their team of volunteers who checked the routes.

First published in 2021 by Alyn Books, Cilcain, Flintshire CH75PD
2nd edition published in 2022
www.alynbooks.com
E-mail:lorna.jenner@btinternet.com
For trade and sales enquiries, please call 01352 741676

Contents

Introducing the Shropshire Hills

Snuggling against the convoluted border of mid-Wales, Shropshire is unassumingly famed as one of the loveliest counties in England. It is a region of variety and contrast, with unspoiled landscapes segueing gently from subtly rolling lowland plains spilling out of Cheshire to the diverse ranges of hills that rumple the skyline to the south. Despite Shropshire's closeness to the industrial Midlands heartland, there are only two towns of any size. These between them account for almost half the population, and the rest of the county remains one of the most sparsely populated areas in England. Away from the few main roads, quiet lanes meander unhurriedly between a scattering of small market towns, picturesque hamlets and farming settlements, while the largely arable fields of the plains give way to grazing pastures, wooded valleys, forests and the unbounded upland heaths of the hills. It is amongst these Shropshire Hills that this book dwells, their stunning beauty formally recognised in 1958, when it became one of the first Areas of Outstanding Natural Beauty (AONB) to be designated in England and Wales.

The diversity of the hills is founded on their underlying geology, the variety of which within such a small geographical area being unequalled anywhere else in the world. The spectrum of rocks represents a period spanning 600 million years of earth's history, pre-dating the dawn of the great explosion of life right up to the present. During that time, the pre-Cambrian roots on which this land rests have migrated north from the Antarctic, while the strata of lime, sand and other sedimentary rocks successively laid down during that journey have been fractured, folded, baked, intruded and eroded by the movement of tectonic plates, volcanism and the weather. That process is ongoing today; the Church Stretton Fault marks a boundary where ancient continents have collided and the ongoing creep continues to cause periodic mini-earthquakes. And while today's weather might not be as dramatic as that of the last glaciation some 15,000 years ago, the elements of wind, water and freeze-thaw continue their subtle moulding of the landscape.

Man too has left his mark. Contours, soil and river patterns determine not only the native vegetation, but also where people live and how they

use the land. The first farmers felled primeval forest to clear space for crops and livestock, with hamlets, villages and towns following in their turn, incrementally creating a pattern of development, interspersed with field, upland, wood and forest. While the result is unquestionably an area of outstanding beauty, the present cloak of vegetation and the character of the land has been influenced, if not created, by man. Without constant management, the character of the countryside would quickly revert to something else, not necessarily better or worse, but certainly quite different.

The Shropshire Hills AONB extends over some 800 square kilometres/310 square miles, covering almost a quarter of the county. It is a gentle landscape, the highest point on Brown Clee Hill only touching 540m. Yet, the hills are not without challenge, for many of the tops demand a steep climb or descent. And while there are no lofty peaks, rugged escarpments, rocky tors and fractured outcrops abound. Many tops can be attained by just a short walk, and adding one to another gives scope for longer days. But do not underestimate these seemingly benign hills, for although the terrain might seem innocuous, winter weather on exposed tops can become ferocious and disorienting mist can creep from nowhere. On a fine day, the views everywhere are far-reaching, taking in a panoramic backdrop from the mountains of Wales to the Cotswolds, Malvern Hills and the hills rising in the Midlands. Looking further north, the Peak District comes into view.

The Shropshire Hills comprise seven distinct and separate groups, each having their own individual character. In the south east, the Clee Hills lay claim to the highest ground, their several main tops almost perfectly aligned north-south. Capped with hard dolerite, they have resisted nature's erosion, and rise as great humps of moorland that suggest an air of abandonment and remoteness. Forming an extensive catchment that feeds the Clun, Redlake and Teme rivers, the gently rounded tops of the Clun Hills regard each other across winding and often deserted valleys. They lie beside the county's border with Wales and it is here that you will find some of the finest stretches of Offa's Dyke. Many of the hills to the east of Clun are cloaked in modern forest plantation and woodland, but oddly those to the west, which once lay within the ancient Clun Forest, are now largely bare. To the north east are the parallel ranges of Shropshire's most frequented hills, The Stiperstones and The Long Mynd. Their sedimentary rocks have been pushed up on end, creating a fine ridge and long plateau, each draped in splendid colourful heath. To the east of the Church Stretton Fault, the rocks of the Stretton Hills are volcanic in origin, the debris thrown out by ancient eruptions rather than the volcanoes themselves. Beyond Ape Dale, the beds of long-gone tropical seas and remnants of coral reefs have been pushed up to create the impressive 30-kilometre/19-mile escarpment of Wenlock

Edge. Looking north east yet again, the long panhandle of the AONB reaches out to The Wrekin, a detached outlier that rises dramatically in splendid isolation from all around.

The many habitats of the Shropshire Hills foster an amazing degree of biodiversity. Much of the open upland is grazed by sheep and you will see cattle and Welsh ponies too. Such land management, together with bracken removal and heather and gorse burning maintains a vibrant heath and moorland. Elsewhere, pockets of unimproved and marginal farmland remain, where species-rich acid grasslands and hay meadows contain less common and rare wild flowers and other plants. Lower down, although cultivated or grass fields contain few species, the bounding hedgerows and walls, scattered trees and small woodland copses are often mini-oases of plant and insect diversity. Large areas of planted conifers might shelter few flowers within their shade, but the ongoing pattern of clear felling creates sudden spurges of wild colour. Semi-natural woodland cloaking slopes too steep for farming or lying beside rivers and streams provides more opportunities for wild life, harbouring spring and early summer flowers as well as countless ferns, fungi, mosses and lichens. And while there are no natural large bodies of water in the hills, there are plenty of small pools and ponds about. Elsewhere, flowing water creates its own bountiful habitats; in the uplands, wet flushes surround emerging springs and seeps while lower down are the thickly vegetated banks of countless streams and rivers.

Wandering quietly, you might come across occasional deer, while foxes, badgers and bats are plentiful. Otters are to be found along some stretches of river and there are plenty of small rodents scurrying about in the long grass and leaf litter. Such diversity of habitat attracts huge numbers of birds, from buzzard, red kite and raven down to small woodland and hedgerow birds. Insects abound too, with butterflies and moths (and their caterpillars) as well as dragonflies and bees those most likely to capture your attention.

Although the hills may seem quiet today, man's presence has been a constant factor since prehistoric times. Ancient trackways such as the Kerry Ridgeway and Portway followed the spines of the hills, embracing their ups and downs in preference to the thickly wooded lowlands and waterlogged valleys. These early arteries carried trade in high value stone and metal tools and ornaments and were a conduit for people spreading ideas and new skills. The tracks are still tramped today, perhaps the oldest products of man's labour to have remained in continuous use. Dotted across the landscape are many monuments in the form of cairns, tumuli and a surviving stone circle. Some served as burials and were perhaps places of communal ritual, while others might have been tribal markers to emphasise belonging and status. Elsewhere, ancient earthworks and ditches defined boundaries of settlement or perhaps marked the limit of clan lands.

With the development of iron, a growing population and competition for resources created new pressures on society and it is during this period that the many hillforts were built. Yet most, it seems, were much more than purely defensive, and encompassed thriving villages with houses, communal buildings and food stores. The large hillfort on the top of The Wrekin is thought to have been the capital of the Cornovii people, a Celtic tribe whose lands extended well beyond the confines of modern-day Shropshire. Surrounded by deep ditches and high embankments that supplemented the hill's natural defences, the forts represent a culmination of formidable skills in planning, organisation and construction. They were obviously not built overnight, but rather the product of many generations, each repairing, adding to or improving what had gone before.

When the Romans arrived in Britain, some tribes acceded to the new rule more or less willingly. However, others held out in spirited defiance, fighting last ditch battles to defend their hilltop eyries. At some sites, archaeologists have found traces of burnt-out huts as well as Roman arrow and spear heads, and there is more than one hill named Caer Caradog, remembering Caratacus's legendary last stand against the

Caer Caradoc

invaders. The Cornovii were amongst those who held out to the end, and their fort on top of The Wrekin is one of several that appear to have been eventually overwhelmed.

The occupation brought a new civilisation, linked by a network of efficient, paved roads. The Roman Watling Street passed through the Stretton Gap from the south to their town at Virconium (Wroxeter), which was named for the Cornovii and became the fourth largest settlement in Roman Britain. Other evidence of their colonisation has been found in the several villas dotted across the countryside, as well as the extensive Roman lead workings at Snailbeach. Rich veins of lead ore outcrop at several places along The Stiperstones and were perhaps a major reason for the Roman interest in the area.

There are few records to tell the history of the period immediately following the Roman's departure from Britain, but life went on for the native Britons until the arrival of the Angles and Saxons. They gradually retreated west towards the Welsh hills in the face of the newcomers and ironically, it is they who became known as the 'foreigners' or Welsh. Saxon settlements sprang up, often around a simple church that itself was based on an earlier sacred site. During the 8th century, the Mercian King Offa defined the western frontier of his kingdom with a long dyke, a border that has largely been followed throughout subsequent history. In the 11th century however, the Normans, buoyed by their success at Hastings, were determined to push their boundaries into the territories of the Welsh princes. But the terrain and dogged determination of the Welsh was against them and the borderlands became a battle zone under the rule of powerful Marcher Lords, who built a series of castles to defend and control the area. But military conquest on its own was rather pointless and in its wake they established new towns, bringing in settlers to work the land and develop trade. Despite the relative peace following Edward I's eventual conquest, Welsh resistance only finally died at the beginning of the 15th century with the failure of Owain Glyndŵr's rebellion.

During the Middle Ages, farming, sheep and trade helped bring stability and prosperity to the area. Mining also began to develop as an industry, leading to the reopening of the Roman lead workings on The Stiperstones and developing quarries, coal and iron mines elsewhere. During the 17th century, industry expanded along the Ironbridge Gorge on a scale never seen before. It created an insatiable demand for charcoal, which was used to smelt iron ore and much of the ancient woodland in the area still bears traces of coppicing. With the development of coke-fired blast furnaces at the beginning of the 18th century, coal mining began in earnest and the seams exploited in the Clee Hills were the highest in the country. As the Industrial Revolution gathered pace during the following century, quarrying too became an important activity in the region, supplying stone for massive building projects such as the docks at Cardiff and the paving of roads in the rapidly expanding manufacturing towns and cities.

Yet, despite its proximity to the industrial Midlands, the arrival of the Shropshire Canal into Shrewsbury and Coalport and the subsequent spread of the railway network, Shropshire stayed relatively isolated from the rest of the country. Apart from the localised exploitation of its minerals, outside Ironbridge Gorge, industrial ventures were few and far between and the county remained largely rural. As the 19th century rumbled on, the special qualities of this unspoiled idyll became recognised in their own right, and the area around Church Stretton began to develop as a Victorian resort, an escape from the grime and noise of the factories.

Since then, there has been inevitable change, but apart from the expansion of Telford and the county town of Shrewsbury, the open space, peace and tranquillity of the Shropshire countryside has become its greatest asset. The AONB may attract around half a million visitors a year, but there are miles enough of footpath, quiet track, lane and unbounded moor for people to explore and you do not have to go far off the beaten track to seemingly have the place to yourself.

The Walks

Whether new to 'walking' or an old hand, these routes are a superb introduction to Shropshire's hills. Icons like The Wrekin and Long Mynd stand beside equally rewarding objectives such as Abdon Burf and Bucknell Hill. Elsewhere, the prehistoric Portway and Offa's Dyke follow footsteps of ancient history, with the hill forts of Caer Caradoc and Bury Ditches remaining impressive achievements of our ancestors. Stone henges at Mitchell's Fold and medieval castles at Clun and Stokesay are other tangible links with history. Shropshire's agricultural heritage is dramatically portrayed at Acton Scott, while Snailbeach and Titterstone Clee reveal an industrial past. Every walk reveal the area's abundant flora and fauna and inspiring views abound. The routes largely follow clear paths, tracks and trods (fainter grassy ways). Ups and downs are occasionally steep, but short lived, and with a modicum of 'map sense', navigation in clear weather should not be a problem.

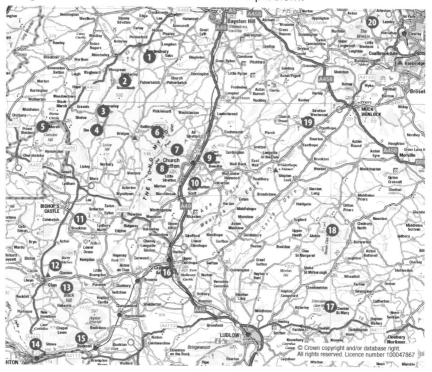

Walk 1 **Earl's Hill**

A distant view and then close encounter with the 'Sleeping Dragon' of Shropshire

What to expect:

Generally good paths and tracks; a couple of steep ascents onto the hills

Distance/time: 6.4km/4 miles. Allow 2 to 2½ hours
Start: Pontesford Hill car park, signed from A488 just east of Pontesbury
Grid ref: SJ 409057
Ordnance Survey map: Explorer 241 (Shrewsbury)
Refreshments: The Nags Head on the A488 between Pontesford and Pontesbury
Transport: 552/553, Shrewsbury to Bishop's Castle stops at Pontesbury

Walk outline

From the car park below the northern foot of Pontesford Hill, the walk first crosses the valley onto the wooded flanks of Oaks Hill, from which there is a distant view to the Sleeping Dragon. After wandering south, there is then a strenuous direct ascent of Earl's Hill, continuing over the summit and down the spine of Pontesford Hill back to the start.

Earl's Hill

Earl's Hill, Shropshire's 'Sleeping Dragon', might not be particularly high but it demands a sharp pull to the summit from all directions. However, the effort is well repaid, for the view across the surrounding countryside is spectacular. The rocks from which the hill is formed are amongst the oldest in Shropshire, hard volcanic lavas, tuff and dolerite intrusions laid down over 650 million years ago. Overlain by subsequent sedimentation, subject to folding and stripped bare again, the hill's present shape was finally sculpted by scouring ice sheets and the subsequent deluge of glacial meltwater. An eternity might have passed and the 'dragon' may now be sleeping, but it lies beside one of the county's major fault lines and occasional twitches can produce discernible earthquakes, like that which affected nearby Bishop's Castle in 1990.

Iron Age defences

The hill boasts two impressive Iron Age defences, the larger straddling some 550m of the summit ridge and would have accommodated a substantial community. The second is much smaller and sits on a flattened shelf at the northern foot of the hill. They date from around 700 BC, although the site of the northern defence has yielded traces of worked flint that suggest there was also a much earlier occupation during Neolithic times. The long continuity of settlement in the area was further reinforced when a stone mould that was used for casting five different sizes of bronze axe was found in the stream at Whalleybourne in 1961.

A great battle

Earl's Hill is reputedly the site of a great battle between the West Saxons and the King of Mercia, which took place at Easter AD 661. During the encounter, one of the kings lost a golden arrow. It was said that whoever found it would receive great wealth. As with such tales, there was an impossible catch – it had to be found before dawn on Palm Sunday by a young maiden, the seventh daughter of a seventh son. During the 19th century, folk came to picnic on the hill and play boisterous games surrounding an arrow hunt. Author Mary Webb, who lived for a short time in Pontesbury, further popularised the myth in her romantic novel entitled 'The Golden Arrow'.

Pontesbury

After the Iron Age, the focus of settlement moved away from the hill. The Romans built a road to their lead mines at Stiperstones through the valley and there was at least one villa close by. The Anglo-Saxons may have given Pontesbury its name and the surrounding fertile land helped the settlement thrive throughout the medieval period. Later on, mining for coal and metal ore as well as quarrying brought further expansion and it became one of the biggest villages in the area. That prosperity was expressed in the magnificent church, almost cathedralic in proportion and standing in the middle of an unusually large graveyard. By the end of the 18th century, the medieval building was showing its age and by 1825, the tower had collapsed, bringing the nave and aisle down with it. Following some argument as to how it should be replaced, the church was rebuilt in the Early English style, echoing the old building.

A nature reserve

In 1962, much of the hill was incorporated within the Shropshire Wildlife Trust's first reserve, and a particular delight in spring is the profusion of bluebells that carpet the ancient woodland. The woodland, parts of which date back hundreds of years, encourages breeding birds such as warblers, tree creepers, jays and woodpeckers, while wildflowers such as heath speedwell and wild thyme on the open meadowland attract a variety of butterflies that include orange tips and small blues.

Jay

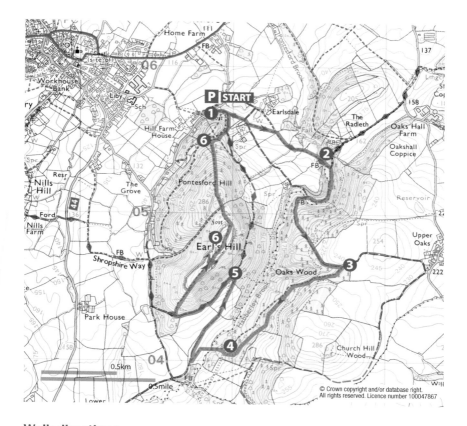

Walk directions

1 Follow the track through a barrier at the rear of the car park. Where it forks, take the left branch and almost immediately drop sharp left to a gate. Strike half-right across a field, dropping out at the far side onto a track. Follow it right a few steps before leaving through a kissing gate on the left.

Walk half-right to another kissing gate by a power-cable post and maintain the same direction in a second, larger field. Through a small, waymarked gate, carry on beside the left hedge, passing through more gates to put the boundary on your right. Over a stile, bear left across a final field to a kissing gate into a wood. A path descends steeply through the trees, passing through more gates to a bridge over Pontesford Brook.

2 Climb beyond to meet a broader path and follow it right. Reaching a second bridge, re-cross the brook. Go left and continue upstream. After 250m, branch left at a fork to find a bridge taking the way once more across the brook.

The ongoing path climbs steadily through Oaks Wood, occasional breaks in the trees giving a view across to Earl's Hill. Eventually meeting a T-junction, go right. Bear left through a broad turning space and carry on within the upper perimeter of the wood.

3 Reaching a waymarked junction, swing right with the main track, which soon begins a long, gradual descent between the trees.

4 Eventually, after a 1.2km the track bends left towards a gate at the edge of the wood. However, leave the track on the bend to follow a narrow path that winds ahead down to a bridge over Habberley Brook (the same stream encountered earlier, but here with a different name).

Climb to a kissing gate into a rough field. Keep ahead past a large oak and then bear right to the top boundary. A trod leads away to the right, passing through a field gate and across a second field to a small gate in the far-left corner. Walk up beyond to a crossing path.

5 To the left, it undulates through a wooded strip around the southern flank of Earl's Hill. After 500m and beyond a bridleway gate, look for a path leaving up right to a stile. Breaking from the trees, it climbs steeply up the southern rib of the hill. Broaching the outer defences of the Iron Age fort, the trig column appears ahead. An easing gradient gives an enjoyable final approach, which passes through a second set of earthworks to reach the top.

6 After savouring the view, continue with the onward path, which drops abruptly through the northern defences to a broad saddle that links it to Pontesford Hill. Over a stile, the trail continues easily through larch plantation, shortly dropping more steeply and eventually meeting a broad, sunken track.

7 The wooded embankment opposite is part of a second, smaller fort, which can be entered a short distance to the left. However, the way back lies to the right. The track curves down below a steep bank, joining with another track from the right to return you to the car park.

Walk 2 **Snailbeach**

Explore the surface remains of Shropshire's largest lead mining complex and visit miners' cottages perched on the hill above

What to expect:
Undulating paths and tracks; a sustained, steady climb during the second half of the walk

Distance/time: 10.1km/6¼ miles. Allow 3½ - 4 hours
Start: Snailbeach Village Hall car park (honesty box)
Grid ref: SJ 372022
Ordnance Survey map: Explorer 216 (Welshpool & Montgomery)
Refreshments: The Mytton Arms at Habberley or The Stiperstones Inn

Walk outline
After winding through the complex site of the Snailbeach lead mine, the walk climbs over the wooded hill behind to the tiny village of Habberley. The way then rises around the southern flank of the hill before climbing to Blakemoorgate, where ancient holy trees and restored miners' cottages beg investigation. The return skirts the impressive fold of Crowsnest Dingle before dropping back to the mine.

The Stiperstones lead mines

Stiperstones lead was first mined by the Romans in the first century AD. A massive pig (ingot of metal) bearing the inscription IMP HADRIAN AVG was found at a nearby farm in 1796, and the ancient workings were still visible above Snailbeach in the middle of the 19th century.

The deposits were intermittently worked again from the early medieval period, but it was not until the latter part of the 18th century that they began to be exploited on a major scale. Expansion increased after the Snailbeach Company was formed in 1783, and the company opened a coal mine and smelt mill near Pontesbury. The ore was initially lifted by horse gin. Power to drain the mine came from a waterwheel, but around 1790 a drainage adit was dug from the 112 yard level to take water out to the Hope Valley. In 1793, to enable deeper mining, the first steam engine was brought in to lift water. A much deeper adit was later begun from Minsterley, but although it was never completed, new deposits of galena (lead ore) were discovered, so the effort was not wasted.

By the middle of the 19th century, the mines employed over 500 people and had become the most productive in the country. A tramway took the ore from the mine to the crushing machines and dressing floors, and a new smelt mill was built, the flue extending up the hill so that lead could condense from the gases. In 1873, the Snailbeach District Railway was opened to connect the mines to the main line at Pontesbury. In addition to carrying lead, it also took out stone from nearby quarries at Eastridge and later Callow Hill, bringing back coal to power the mines' steam engines.

But within ten years, the price of lead began to fall and, after losses in 1884, the company was liquidated and reopened on a much smaller scale. The operation became increasingly unprofitable. By 1895, the smelt mill had closed and the mine followed in 1913. Yet, that was not the end. From 1900, the tailings (mining waste) were worked for fluorspar and the upper levels of the mine were reopened during the Second World War for the production of barytes. The mine finally closed for good in 1955, although surface working continued into the 1970s. Today, what remains of the mine workings, both above and below ground are some of the most complete of their kind in the country. Much work has been undertaken to consolidate and preserve them and they are opened to visitors during the summer.

Ancient holly trees and a hillside mining settlement

The route from Lordshill up to Blakemoorgate passes a rare survival, a grove of ancient holly trees, some of which may be 400 years old. A slow growing evergreen, holly has become inextricably linked with Christmas, but during the Middle Ages was an important source of fodder for over-wintering livestock. Groves of holly were managed by pollarding, the upper leaves being relatively spineless and quite nutritious. As the Industrial Revolution got underway, most were cut down for their wood, which was used in the manufacture of bobbins for the rapidly growing textile industry. That they survived here is perhaps indirectly due to the mines, since some of the workers settled on the hill and used the trees to feed their animals.

Fieldfare

Cottage at Blakemoorgate

Gnarled, split and wizened, many of the trunks look all but dead, yet new growth springs from cracked bark to bear bright leaves and deep red berries. After the first frosts, the berries are a favourite food of fieldfares and redwings, some of whom may have previously feasted on rowan berries and leave a small 'deposit' before they fly on. Wrapped in their packet of fertiliser, the rowan seeds have taken root in the cracks and crevices and, in growing, may even split the host trunk apart. While the hollies appear well able to survive this, they are vulnerable to sheep that will nibble at new growth and rub away the bark, hence the need for the fencing around the trees.

Just up the hill from The Hollies is Blakemoorgate, a small settlement built around the beginning of the 19th century by miners working over in Snailbeach. Using local stone and clay rather than mortar, the cottages were built into the lee of the hillside to gain shelter from the prevailing weather; further protection came from the planted grove of trees. The spot was chosen perhaps because of a nearby spring, with gorse being cleared to create small fields for grazing livestock or small allotments. Despite the harsh conditions, these dwellings remained occupied until the 1950s and some have since been restored as a heritage project.

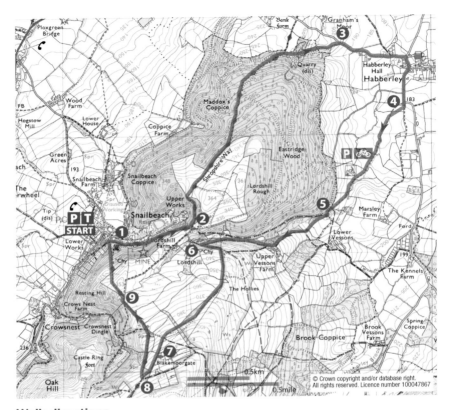

Walk directions

1 Leave the lane opposite the parking through a kissing gate past old mine workings. Rejoining the lane, keep on the main branch, winding past cottages and along the side of the wooded valley.

2 Higher up, reaching a sharp bend, bear off left with the Shropshire Way. Continue within the trees and then along the right-hand boundary of a field before resuming at the edge of the forest. The path later turns into the thick of the wood, descending to a junction. Go right, with the permissive bridleway. Ignore a footpath off left, but then bear left at a junction shortly after. The track finally emerges past a barrier onto a lane.

3 Walk downhill to Habberley, there turning right towards Cumberbatch and Bridges. At the next fork, the Mytton Arms lies to the left, just past the church. The onward route, however, is to the right. Leaving the village, pass a lane off to the right and continue a little farther to a bend.

4 Leave ahead along a short track, passing through a gate at its end into a field. Follow the left hedge into a second field and then bear right, keeping left of two ash trees to find a waymarked gate at the far side. Cross a stream and swing left to a kissing gate and footbridge in the corner. Keep going beside the stream until you enter the fourth field and there strike away to a gate hidden in the far corner leading into Eastridge Wood.

5 Walk forward to a metalled track and go left. At a fork, keep left again, following the track through a gate out of the trees and on up to Upper Vessons Farm. Approaching barns, swing right and then keep right as the track forks, the way soon rising along the valley side and eventually meeting a junction below a brick chimney.

6 Turn sharp left and continue climbing, the way shortly curving right up a more open hillside dotted here and there with clumps of ancient holly. Soon after passing through a belt of pine, the trail enters the Stiperstones National Nature Reserve. Walk on a little farther to find a gate on the left, leading to the restored Blakemoregate cottages.

7 Return to the main track and continue up the hill, passing through a gate onto the open moor.

8 At a waypost, just past a track joining from the left, double back right on a descending path that arcs above Crowsnest Dingle. Through a gate, the way winds on at the edge of rough pasture. Before long, the way turns away, leaving the nature reserve through a gate.

9 Walk away half-left, passing left of the high point and then dropping to a kissing gate at the bottom, near a chimney that rises from the trees. The ongoing path drops steeply through the wood, passing a path off right to the chimney. Continue downhill, taking the right branch at a fork to wind past more mining ruins and finally emerge beside the mine entrance. After exploring the site, return along the main lane back to the car park.

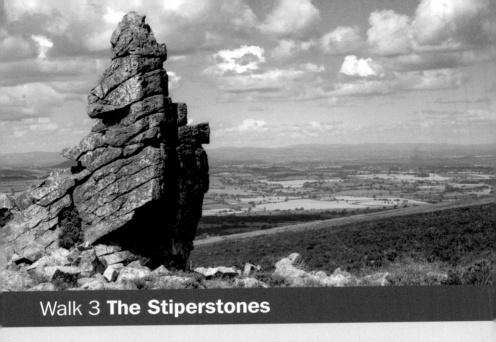

Walk 3 **The Stiperstones**

A superb walk along one of Shropshire's most dramatic hills

What to expect:

Generally good paths and tracks with short stretches on a quiet lane; steep ascents and descents

Distance/time: 8.9km/5½ miles. Allow 3½ to 4 hours
Start: The Bog car park, south of Stiperstones
Grid ref: SO 357978
Ordnance Survey map: Explorer 216 (Welshpool & Montgomery)
Refreshments: Café at the Bog Centre or The Stiperstones Inn
Transport: The Bog Centre and Stiperstones are served by The Long Mynd and Stiperstones Shuttle bus

Walk outline

The walk begins with an easy climb to the low saddle separating Nipstone Rock from the main Stiperstones ridge. Turning north east, it gradually ascends past the outcrops dominating the skyline before falling to Blakemoor Flat. There follows a steep descent through Mytton Dingle to Stiperstones village, with its welcoming pub. After a short stretch along a lane, there is a steep pull back onto the moor above Perkins Beach, finally contouring the lower slopes before dropping back to The Bog.

The Stiperstones ridge

The Stiperstones ridge is one of the most startling landscape features of the Shropshire Hills. Running for over 8km/5 miles, the ground drops steeply on either side, while dramatic, bristling tors intermittently punctuate the length of its spine. The long summit ridge is the exposed end of an upended stratum of quartzite, a hard, resistant rock formed from ancient sandstones that have been folded and metamorphosed by the subterranean heat and pressure generated by the incessant creep of the earth's tectonic plates. During the last glacial period, the top of the ridge remained above the surrounding ice sheet, but was subject to seasonal freeze and thaw, which shattered the rock into sharp boulders and fragments. During warmer periods, the upper layer of permafrost melted, and the waterlogged mass gradually crept downhill taking the rocky debris with it, creating the 'stone flows' that are such a prominent feature.

Rising to 536m, the ridge is the second highest feature in the county, the culmination being Manstone Rock on which there is a trig column. The Devil's Chair, just a little to the north, however, is the more massive outcrop and is steeped in a host of malevolent legends that feed off the sometimes other-worldly mists and clouds that can engulf the tops. Some tales credit the Devil or his witches with dumping the piles of rocks perhaps to build a demonic castle, or else have him enthroned on the chair at the winter solstice carousing with his malicious followers. The Stiperstones ridge itself, together with that of The Long Mynd to the east are said to be the corpses of two great dragons, one white (symbolising England)and the other red (the Welsh Dragon), which fought a dire battle in the skies above that ultimately brought their mutual destruction. Other melancholic legends surround the ghost of a Saxon nobleman, who is said to gallop across the hills with his ethereal army when the country is threatened with invasion.

But, despite the forbidding legends, the ridge has long been a focus for settlement. Four ancient cairns, a Bronze Age long barrow and a defended Iron Age enclosure are scattered along the top. More recently, when the lower hills were mined for lead, squatting miners looking for somewhere to live built rude cottages on the common ground of the higher slopes. One small group of cottages has been restored as a heritage exhibition (see walk 2) while another has been taken over as a monastic hermitage.

Like limestone, weathering quartzite produces little soil or nutrient, which has left the ground impoverished. Nevertheless, early farmers colonised the area and traces of ancient field systems have been identified. The hill's management as hay meadow and grazing kept the uplands clear of woodland encroachment, but such environments are becoming rare, threatened by changing agricultural practices during the 20th century. Soil improvement, re-seeding, conifer planting and under- or over-grazing all impinge upon these fragile environments, hastening the disappearance of the often rare plants that thrive on these poor soils. In the 1960s much of the area was designated a National Nature Reserve and steps taken to reverse the losses. The removal of conifer plantations and restoration of heath and herb-rich grassland is showing some success in restoring diversity and opening long lost views, while Hebridean sheep and Exmoor ponies are used for sympathetic grazing to maintain the open heath.

Plants such plants as heather, cowberry, whimberry and mountain pansy are making a comeback, with bog asphodel, cotton grass and marsh violet

Cowberry

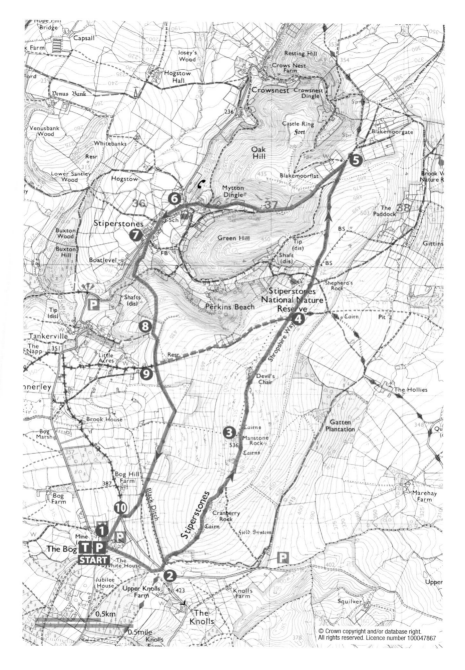

in the wet flushes. Curlew, skylark, meadow pipit and red grouse are to be seen in the skies while brown hare, fox and common lizard can all be spotted. Insects abound too, particularly butterflies, encouraged by flower-rich hay meadows.

Walk directions

1 Leave the top of the car park by a signpost, following the Shropshire Way south past a pond. At a second waypost, keep left on a narrow path through bracken. Go right at the end up steps to a kissing gate and walk away by the right boundary. Through another kissing gate at the top, bear left to a gate, which opens onto a lane.

2 Cross to a gate opposite, continuing through a second gate onto the moor. Keep ahead at a fork, but take the left branch a little farther on. Climb gently across the moor, passing the first of the Stiperstones outcrops towards Cranberry Rock. Beyond that, the main path follows the spine of the ridge, steadily rising onwards towards the high point of Manstone Rock. The trig column is perched on top of the tor and can only be reached by a scramble.

3 Carry on along the ridge, passing the Devil's Chair and eventually reaching a waypost at a crossing of paths.

4 To shorten the walk, the path left offers an easy return without losing any unnecessary height. Follow it gently downhill for 1.2km to the edge of the moor to rejoin the main route at Point (9).

Otherwise, keep ahead, shortly reaching a crosspath near the Shepherd's Rock. Again keep ahead, now on a broad gravel path. The way continues easily down, giving dramatic views into the deep valleys either side of Green Hill. Carry on for 800m until you meet the corner of an old boundary coming in from the left.

5 Turn back sharp left beside it on a grass track. After 250m, as it curves towards Oak Hill, bear off left at a fork and then keep right at a second fork. Initially stepped, the path drops sharply into the head of Mytton Dingle. Below the steps, the gradient eases, the path finally broadening to run out along the valley past abandoned mine workings. Keep right with the main path, leaving the nature reserve past a memorial to the crew of a Whitley bomber that crashed into the hillside on 15th February 1944. Carry on past cottages to emerge onto a lane in Stiperstones.

6 Walk left past the Stiperstones Inn, continuing for 500m through the village.

7 At the far end, some 25m past the last cottage on the left, look for a footpath signed off on the left. It climbs back to a stile behind the cottage. Head steeply uphill at the field edge, occasionally pausing to appreciate the views back across the foot of Green Hill. Near the top corner, a waymark directs you left to a stile at the edge of a wood. Continue climbing ahead through the trees. Eventually the wood thins, and the gradient eases across open ground to a stile.

8 Over the stile, bear left across rough pasture to a gate at the far corner. Emerging onto a track, follow it right at the edge of the open moor.

9 At a post, a path joins from the left, the short cut from the ridge. Keep ahead, with the track, passing through occasional gates for some 1.2km/¾ mile. Eventually, the Bog Centre comes into view below ahead and the track becomes enclosed. Keep going, ultimately turning down to a final gate.

10 Walk left to the lane and follow it right back to the car park.

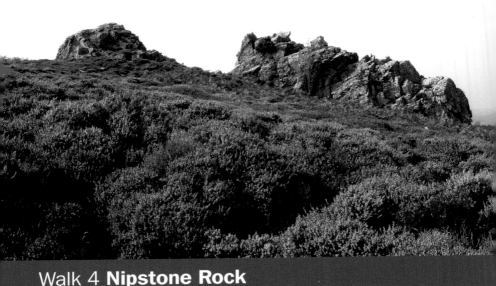

Walk 4 **Nipstone Rock**

This is one of Shropshire's unsung gems - an undemanding walk onto an outlier of the Stiperstones ridge.

What to expect:
Clear paths and tracks through woodland, heath and pasture

Distance/time: 4km/2½ miles. Allow 1 to 1½ hours
Start: The Bog car park, south of Stiperstones
Grid ref: SO 357978
Ordnance Survey map: Explorer 217 (The Long Mynd & Wenlock Edge)
Refreshments: Seasonal café at the Bog Centre
Transport: The Bog Centre is served by The Long Mynd and Stiperstones Shuttle bus

Walk outline
Beginning beside the scant pithead ruins of the old Bog Mine, the route contours the lower slopes of the Nipstone ridge through wetland wood and pasture before climbing onto the open heath above. The high ground is easily gained, opening panoramic views for the return leg.

An old lead mine

As suggested by its name, the car park area was once a marsh, but subsequently drained in the 18th century to make way for lead mining. A rich seam of ore underlay the western flank of the Stiperstones ridge and the Bog Mine was one of the earliest industrial ventures to exploit it. Work began around 1730, primarily extracting lead, but yielding zinc and silver too. Over time, three shafts were sunk. However, the workings were prone to flooding and profit often remained elusive. Yet, despite periodic closure and several changes of ownership, there was also significant investment. In 1777, one of Boulton and Watt's first beam engines was installed to keep the workings dry, and just a decade later, work began on an ambitious adit to act as a sough, which dewatered several mines in the vicinity. This drainage tunnel left the workings some 130m below ground and ran for over 3.2km/2 miles to emerge from the hillside a little north west of Stiperstones village. It brought the added bonus that ore could then be taken out by boat towards the smelt works, which lay near Pontesbury and thus the tunnel became known as the 'Boat Level'. By the end of the 18th century, the mine had been progressively sunk to a depth of around 370m and around 100 men were employed underground. A thriving village grew around the pithead to accommodate them, complete with school, pub and a miners' institute.

By 1890 the ore had largely been exhausted, but the mine was reopened in the early 20th century to extract barytes, a mineral used in the chemical, paint and paper industries. An aerial ropeway took the barytes to Malehurst near Minsterley, over 8km/5 miles away, where it was processed and loaded onto railway wagons. With the First World War, interest in lead was revived and an exploratory tunnel was dug near the present car park in the hope of finding more deposits. However local stories suggest that the exercise was undertaken purely to create work for miners and thus keep them from conscription into the army. It became known as the Somme Tunnel, but failed to find any new ore and the 400-foot adit was eventually taken over as a roost by several species of bat.

The mines finally closed about 1922 and the pit-head buildings were abandoned to the elements. Without employment, the community gradually drifted away and, by 1972, the village had largely been demolished. The Miners Arms was spared, but with its customers gone, has not been a pub since the 1960s. The Institute managed to survive into the '80s, but that too was finally knocked down, leaving only the school, which now serves as a Visitor Centre. But, although only scattered ruins mark the old pit-head, overgrown spoil heaps, former dressing floors, old reservoir pools, a tramline causeway and the powder magazine still portray the extent of the enterprise.

A nature reserve

On the ridge, the walk enters the Nipstone Rock Local Nature Reserve, managed by Shropshire Wildlife Trust. A noted feature is the presence of the large emperor moth, attracted by the heather and whinberry upon which the caterpillars voraciously feed. The female can have a wingspan of 4 inches and is one of the UK's largest and most impressive moths. Even though much of the Stiperstones upland is protected within a National Nature Reserve, many areas along the ridge were planted with conifers during the 1960s. This disruption of the open heath affected the moth populations and an ongoing project is focused on clearing conifers to create a continuous corridor along which the moths can once again spread. Such open terrain also favours grayling butterflies, which are superbly camouflaged and difficult to spot at rest. Some areas are being replanted with locally native trees such as ash, rowan and oak, which provide a more natural cover for bats and birds. Other species to look out for include curlew, red grouse, meadow pipit and skylark.

Curlew

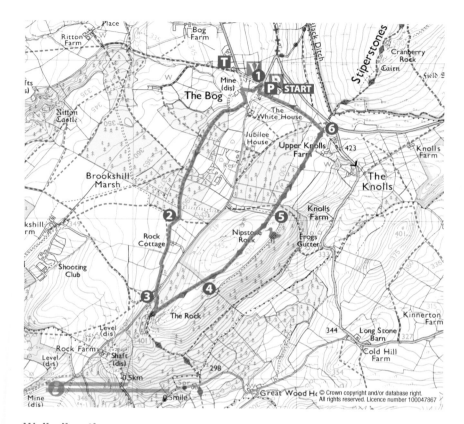

Walk directions

1 Leave the bottom-right corner of the car park to a lane opposite the site of the Bog Mine,and briefly follow it left a short distance to a waymarked track leaving on the right. Continue through a gate/stile beside a marshy pool, soon reaching a second gate into a wood. Follow the track ahead through the trees, eventually meeting an intersecting track. Continue forward along a narrow path at the edge of the wood, shortly leaving through a gate.

2 With the remnants of a fence on your left, keep ahead towards Rock Cottage. Over to the right, the ground folds into the tributary valleys of the River West Onny. Beyond the cottage, walk ahead through a gap and on with an old hedge boundary on your right. Through a gate at the far end, press on along a narrowing pasture, leaving beyond a crossing track through a gate on the left back onto the lane.

3 Cross to another gate from which an indistinct path slants right across the heath towards Nipstone Rock. Meeting another path below the foot of the broken rocks at a Shropshire Way marker, turn sharp left and climb gently across the slope to the crest of the ridge. In late summer the heather hums with bees, while the twigs of the whimberries are heavy with juicy fruit. Gaining the crest walk forward to a gate in a lateral fence.

4 Through that, carry on along the ridge path to top the rise, shortly passing the isolated Nipstone Rock on your left.

5 Through a gate, walk forward over a crossing track towards the corner of a wood. There, a kissing gate takes you out of the Nipstone Rock Local Nature Reserve. Walk on within the fringe of trees, emerging beyond to follow the line of an old boundary across grazing.

6 Reaching a signpost in the middle of the field, turn left to a gate. Keep the same direction down the next field to a kissing gate, from which a stepped path drops to the right. At the bottom, the path ahead leads through to a viewpoint, but the way back is to the left. Meeting open ground, go right past a small pond and then left to return to the car park.

Walk 5 Mitchell's Fold Stone Circle and Corndon Hill

Straddling the English/Welsh border, hilltop burial cairns and a stone circle make this a hill walk with a difference

What to expect:
Generally clear paths and tracks; a couple of steep ascents

Distance/time: 7.7km/4¾ miles. Allow 3 to 3½ hours
Start: Small parking area at end of track near Mitchell's Fold Stone Circle
Grid ref: SO 302980
Ordnance Survey map: OS Explorer 216 (Welshpool & Montgomery)
Refreshments: The Miners Arms, Priest Weston
Transport: None

Walk outline

Leaving the parking near Mitchell's Fold, the route returns to the lane for a strenuous climb onto the top of Cordon Hill. After exploring the burial cairns dotting the summit, the way drops off the steep western flank to Priest Weston, where a pub offers refreshment. The return rises along the neighbouring valley of Cwm Dingle, climbing steeply out at its head to the stone circle and back to the start.

Bronze Age relics

Shropshire's hills have attracted man since the earliest times and the area around Cordon Hill is no exception. Archaeological study has revealed that the area was cleared of its original native woodland for agriculture during the Neolithic period. A probable 'axe factory' has been identified just south of the hill at Cwm Mawr near Hyssington where there is an outcrop of picrite, an extremely hard stone that was ideal for the production of axe heads. Almost 100 examples of hafted axe hammers and 'battle axes' fashioned from Cwm Mawr stone have been found up and down the country, suggesting that there was a significant industry here some 4,500 years ago. The area lay close to the prehistoric Kerry and Clun-Clee ridgeways, along which the axes could have been transported for trade.

Other evidence of ancient settlement is the many Bronze Age burial cairns scattered around Corndon Hill. The prominent pile of stones beside the trig column on the summit is one, with two more on the spur to the south west, the larger being around 23m diameter. The hollows excavated within them are modern and serve as shelters from the weather.

Other relics from the same period include three stone circles. The most impressive, Mitchell's Fold is passed towards the end of the walk. It is thought that it originally consisted of more than 30 stones, apparently brought from Stapeley Hill, the higher ground to the north west. Only 15 still stand today but, nevertheless, with a 25m diameter, it remains an impressive structure. The long axis, marked at its south eastern end by a taller stone, apossibly one of an original pair marking the 'entrance' appears to be aligned with the mid-winter moonrise. A slightly smaller circle known as the Hoarstones can be found some 2.4km/1½ miles below the north eastern corner of Stapeley Hill and contains 38 small stones.

The third circle, the Whetstones, was destroyed in the 19th century and is now sadly reduced to a scattering of rubble. Collectively, the various monuments scattered around the hillsides suggest a stable and prosperous community, being able to call on significant resources to construct such an impressive array of ceremonial structures that have remained a dominant feature of the landscape for more than 4,000 years. Yet, despite all the archaeological research that has been undertaken, we can still only guess at their true purpose.

However, as is usually the case, folklore comes galloping to the rescue to fill in the gaps. Way back when, during a time of great hardship, a kindly witch brought a cow that gave unlimited milk. Each villager could come to fill their pail every day and so help them through the famine. But one night, a wicked witch appeared and set about milking the cow into a sieve. Eventually the cow realised what was happening and, so enraged by the waste, bounded off, some say to Dunsmore Heath, where it wrought havoc until it was eventually killed by Guy of Warwick. When the villagers arrived the following morning for their milk, they found the wicked witch turned to stone for her villainy and so erected a palisade of stones around it to ensure she never escaped.

An industrial past

While Priest Weston is in England (only just), Corndon Hill lies across the border in Wales. Until the Dissolution, the tiny hamlet at the foot of the hill formed part of the lands held by the Augustinian priory at nearby Chirbury, where only fragments of the monastic buildings remain in the churchyard. Throughout its history, the area here had been largely agricultural, but in the middle of the 19th century a mine opened to produce barytes, a high density mineral used as a filler in the manufacture of pigments, paper and cloth as well as in the drilling industry. Although the mines closed in 1927, their memory lingers on in the Miner's Arms pub.

Walk directions

1 Walk back along the track to the lane and follow it ahead. Within a few steps, you cross from Shropshire into Powys, from England into Wales. There is little topographically to indicate the boundary, although in the field to the east, it follows the course of a fledgling stream that later becomes the River West Onny and ultimately meets the River Severn near Worcester. Keep with the lane until, some 150m beyond the next bend and shortly after a gate, you will find a stile in the hedge on the right.

2 Head away by the right-hand fence to a stile in the corner and continue over more stiles, gently gaining height across the slope of the hill. Eventually crossing back onto access land, walk forward through bracken to a junction and turn right. The path initially winds back above the fence before turning to tackle the steep slope head-on up to the summit.

3 Having expended so much effort in attaining the top, it is worth striking out left towards a slightly lower satellite summit on which there are the remains of a massive burial cairn.

4 Return to the trig column and continue past, losing height steeply beside a fence on the left bounding an old plantation. Lower down the devastation of broken stumps and brash is relieved by more recent planting. Passing through a gate, drop to a track and go left for 200m.

5 Just after crossing a stream, branch off right to contour the edge of a pasture. Descending into the base of a dip, swing right again along a path that steadily falls through the bracken. Over a stile, keep going down, eventually breaking out onto a lower meadow. A guiding trod leads to a gate beside the sharp bend of a track. Follow it left until you reach stile on right. Cross stile and immediately through gate to enter a field. Go over next stile in the bottom right of field and head down to stile onto lane.

6 Turn left and then fork right at the next junction towards Marton and Chirbury. (To visit The Miners Arms fork right at this junction and then retrace your steps to rejoin the route. This was one of the local pubs

in which Ronnie Lane performed impromptu gigs when he lived nearby during the 1970s.) After 75m, branch off right along a rising track marked as a byway. Approaching a gate into Chapel House, bear right again, still climbing the ancient byway. Eventually emerging onto the bend of a track, keep ahead past houses. However, where it bends left opposite Ceaymanache, leave left through a gate onto a track to Tyn Y-Pistyll, which gently descends to the head of Cwm Dingle.

7 Approaching the end of the track by a green wooden shed, turn off right on a permissive footpath to a stile beside a gate. Over the stile go left and climb steeply though a stand of larch to gain the ridge above. Follow the ridge away to the right, before long reaching a stile onto access land.

8 Swing right on a path rising through bracken to the high point, continuing beyond to a T-junction. Walk left, and carry on over a couple of crossing tracks to find the stone circle.

9 Turn right before it and follow a broad track back down to the car park.

Walk 6 **Ratlinghope and The Portway**

An enjoyable ascent of The Long Mynd from the west, following an ancient trackway along the ridge to return through the pretty valley of Darnford Brook

What to expect:
Generally good paths, tracks and quiet lanes; sustained but not overly steep ascent

Distance/time: 12.1km/7½ miles. Allow 3½ to 4 hours
Start: Car park at Bridges, opposite The Horseshoe Inn
Grid ref: SO 393964
Ordnance Survey map: Explorer 217 (The Long Mynd & Wenlock Edge)
Refreshments: The Horseshoe Inn, Bridges
Transport: The Long Mynd and Stiperstones Shuttle bus

Walk outline
The route follows a lane and then a wooded track before rising out of the valley to Manor House. Back on lanes, the climb continues towards The Long Mynd, shortly crossing the open heath of Wild Moor. There is then an airy stretch following The Portway along the top of The Long Mynd ridge, swinging off above Hawkham Hollow along a high spur to the Betchcott Hills. Dropping into the valley, the return follows Darnford Brook back to Bridges.

Early settlement

As over at Church Stretton, early settlement at Ratlinghope was on the hilltops rather than in the valley, with a couple of enclosed settlements being built above the Darnford Brook valley. The Saxons established a community here, but it remained an out of the way place, and the suffix 'hope' means 'secluded valley'. During the early 13th century, a small cell was founded as a dependency of the Augustine abbey at Wigmore, the black canons enjoying the protection of the Welsh prince Llywelyn ap Iorworth. The community was disbanded at the Dissolution and only scant traces remain beside the present church. Nearby, the old school house has been converted into a YHA hostel, while the pub at Bridges has a fine reputation for its food and hospitality.

An ancient trackway

The Portway along the top of The Long Mynd is an ancient track, possibly of prehistoric origin, which kept to the high ground to avoid the heavily wooded and often marshy lowlands. Local tradition says it was adopted by the Romans and by the 13th century had become a well-used drove road between market towns – the 'ports'. By the 18th century, the road through the Stretton Gap had been improved, but the imposition of a turnpike charge once again pushed traffic onto the hills. It was only during the 19th century development of the railway and eventual metalling of the valley highway that it fell from use to become the quiet trackway it is today.

Winter perils on the hills

On a summer's day, it is hard to imagine how unforgiving the winter can be on the tops. One Sunday in January 1865, the rector of Woolstaston set off for home on his horse from Ratlinghope, having delivered an afternoon service. As he climbed onto Wild Moor, a blizzard set in and, despite knowing the area well, he soon became lost. Floundering through the deep snow, his mount became exhausted and died, but he pressed on through the night and managed to descend into the Cardingmill Valley before collapsing. Luckily, he was found by playing children and taken to shelter where he eventually recovered. Having lived to tell the tale, he was persuaded to publish a pamphlet detailing his ordeal, the proceeds of which he used to furnish the church, and to ensure there was no recurrence of the near-tragedy, the lord of Ratlinghope manor helped provide a vicarage and incumbent for the village.

A fragile habitat

Upland heather heath is an important wildlife habitat, which, although found across north west Europe, is predominantly a British feature. Typified by thin, nutrient-poor, acid soils, it is not a natural landscape, but was cleared of primeval woodland by prehistoric farmers. Its character has been maintained over millennia by light grazing, but since the end of the Second World War, vast swathes have been lost to aforestation and improved grassland. Elsewhere, changing farming practice and overgrazing have led to degradation, yet, abandoned completely, the heath would eventually revert through scrub back to woodland.

Owned by the National Trust since 1965, The Long Mynd is carefully managed to protect this increasingly threatened habitat. Sheep grazing has been reduced in favour of ponies, which do not crop the vegetation as closely, while periodic heather burning encourages new growth, a food source for red grouse. Bracken provides breeding cover for moorland birds and was once harvested for livestock bedding, but if unchecked, quickly proliferates to smother other species. To maintain a balance, it is periodically cut and sold as a substitute for peat.

Red Grouse

The programme is showing success and the late-summer hillsides are once again washed deep purple with flowering heather. Elsewhere, two species of gorse grow together but flower at different times, producing an almost continuous show of bright yellow. The area is famed for whinberries, which grow amongst the heather, producing a harvest of succulent fruit at the end of summer for birds and man alike. Here and there, an isolated wind-bent hawthorn breaks the skyline, some being over 100 years old, but unless specifically protected from nibbling sheep, no new saplings will grow to take their place. The wet flushes surrounding seeping springs have their own plants such as bog asphodel, cotton grass and lady fern, as well as butterwort and sundew, two carnivorous plants that rely on insects for their nourishment. Across the moors, look for wood sorrell (a throwback to the ancient woodland) and common spotted orchid, while grassy slopes harbour heath bedstraw.

Spring and summer is the best time to come for birds, with skylark, wheatear and stonechat to be seen. A rarer sighting is a ring ouzel, but red grouse and curlew are common. Amongst the trees in the valleys, look for pied flycatcher and tree pipit, while by the streams can be found grey wagtail and dipper. The flowering heather attracts countless bees while various butterflies, moths and dragonflies all populate the moor.

© Crown copyright and/or database right.
All rights reserved. Licence number 100047867

Walk directions

1 Leaving the car park, go left to a junction and turn right towards the YHA hostel. After 400m, just before a bridge over Darnford Brook, leave through a kissing gate on the left. Signed 'Shropshire Way', a pleasant wooded track heads upstream. Walk for another 400m to a waymarked junction. Fork right over a bridge and climb away at the edge of a field. At the top, a track leads out beside a cottage to a lane opposite Manor House.

2 Turn left to a junction and there go right towards Belmore and Church Stretton. Walk uphill for 800m before branching off left on a track. However, immediately before a cattle grid, leave over a stile on the right and climb steeply beside the fence. Through a gate at the top corner, cross a track and keep ahead beside a guiding fence at the edge of open moor. Continue beyond its corner, the gradient easing as the path settles across Wild Moor to meet a lane.

3 Briefly join the lane before branching off along the continuing track. Carry on across the moor, after a while cresting the hill to arrive at a T-junction with a broad, gravel track.

4 Turn left, shortly coming to a second junction. Go left again with the Shropshire Way, following The Portway along the ridge. Keep ahead at a later fork, in time reaching a second fork. Again, walk forward, the track soon emerging through a small car park onto a lane.

5 Go right for 300m to find, opposite a small pull-in, a path leaving on the left. Drop down to a farm track and follow it left, winding up to a gate. Walk on beside a plantation, but as the track then swings right, continue ahead beside the right-hand fence, passing through successive gates.

6 Eventually, beyond a shallow dip, facing a choice of gates, take the right-hand one. Carry on, initially between fences. The way continues over the crest of Betchcott Hill, before descending through a gate by a small barn along a fenced track.

7 After 100m, just beyond a gate at the foot of a dip, leave the track through a kissing gate on the left. Signed to Bridges and Stiperstones, a trod falls away along the base of Golden Valley. Continue down over a stile, later watching for the path swinging abruptly right at a waypost. Over a stream, curve left to a stile and gate.

8 Now following the 'Darnford Walk', go left beside the wall. Through another gate, the path drops to a three-way sign near Lower Darnford Farm. Keep right with the Shropshire Way, walking down the valley for almost 1.6km/1 mile and ultimately passing a small quarry to reach a bridge and ford near a farm at the edge of Ratlinghope.

9 Ignore the bridge and instead bear right to a wall stile. The Shropshire Way continues beside a woodland garden, crossing stiles to emerge onto a crossing track. Take the gate opposite and carry on above the Darnford Brook. Reaching a clearing, bear left through a kissing gate back into trees. Walk on past a waymark, reversing your outward route back to Bridges.

Walk 7 **Carding Mill and The Long Mynd**

Carding Mill Valley and The Long Mynd lie at the heart of the Shropshire Hills

What to expect:

Generally good hill paths and tracks; two steep ascents onto the hills.

Distance/time: 9.7km/6 miles. Allow 3½ to 4 hours
Start: Pay and display car park areas in Carding Mill Valley (National Trust)
Grid ref: SO 447943
Ordnance Survey map: Explorer 217 (The Long Mynd & Wenlock Edge)
Refreshments: Café at the Chalet Pavilion (NT) in Carding Mill Valley
Transport: The Long Mynd and Stiperstones Shuttle bus and railway station at nearby Church Stretton

Walk outline

The walk climbs out of Carding Mill Valley onto the shoulder of Stanyeld overlooking Church Stretton. It then follows a clear track through a golf course around the northern flank of Bodbury Hill, detouring to the hill-fort on its summit. The climb continues over Haddon Hill, eventually meeting The Portway along the crest of The Long Mynd. Curving round to the south, the return descends through Lightspout Hollow into Carding Mill Valley, returning to the parking below the Chalet Pavilion.

The Carding Mill Valley

There's a lot more to the Carding Mill Valley than first meets the eye. Although the popularity of Church Stretton and the Carding Mill Valley only developed during the latter part of the 19th century, the area's history stretches back 5,000 years or more.

The oldest 'monument', if you can call it that, is The Portway, first trodden as a seasonal migration or trade route by Neolithic people. Such pathways typically followed high ground to avoid heavily wooded and often marshy valleys, and The Portway runs the length of The Long Mynd, part of a countrywide network of ancient tracks.

Dotting the hills are occasional tumuli or barrows, impressive funerary monuments that may also have served as symbols of tribal status. They indicate settlement during the Bronze Age, a period when farming and the domestication of animals evolved. This brought settled communities and the gradual clearance of the extensive woodland that once covered these now-bare hills. The most obvious prehistoric remains, however, are the Iron Age hill-forts. They appeared from around 800BC, often reusing Bronze Age sites and some 50 are known in Shropshire. Relatively small, but impressively sited above Carding Mill Valley, Bodbury Ring incorporates

punishingly steep hillsides in its defence and was an effective lookout. Their purpose is still debated, with conflicting theories as to whether they were settlement sites or merely refuges in times of trouble. While excavations have often revealed dwellings, the scarcity of hilltop water questions the practicality of permanent occupation. No single answer satisfies every case.

There had been a corn mill in the valley since the 13th century, but in 1812, this was demolished and replaced with a new mill. Powered by tumbling streams, it was soon converted into the carding mill that gave the valley its name. It mechanised the laborious process of turning sheep's fleece into roving, which was then spun into thread as a local cottage industry. More automation came in 1824, when an extension was built to house spinning jennies and hand looms. Eventually, seamstresses were also employed to produce finished garments from the cloth. But, remote from the main wool-producing areas, the factory was hardly profitable and in later years, the mill was demolished and the remaining buildings were put to bottling the aerated spring water that sprang from the hillside and manufacturing ginger beer.

Aspirations of a spa town

By this time, the railway had begun to bring visitors to enjoy the unspoiled countryside. The area had become known as 'Little Switzerland' and Church Stretton aspired to become a spa town. A second spring water bottling plant opened at the foot of Cwm Dale (still operating today) while the new century brought a golf course (the third highest in Britain) and The Longmynd Hotel, which opened as a 'hydro' offering therapeutic water treatments and diets.

Although the ambitions for a spa never really materialised, the town developed to service a growing tourist industry focused on the beautiful Carding Mill Valley. The factory was turned into a hotel and café but was superseded in 1920 when it was converted to flats, and the Chalet Pavilion tearoom was imported as a prefabricated building from Scandinavia.

Since 1965 much of The Long Mynd has been owned by the National Trust, with the Chalet serving as a visitor centre and café. Although Carding Mill Valley has become a honeypot attracting over 250,000 visitors a year, the surrounding hills remain relatively quiet, as this superb walk reveals.

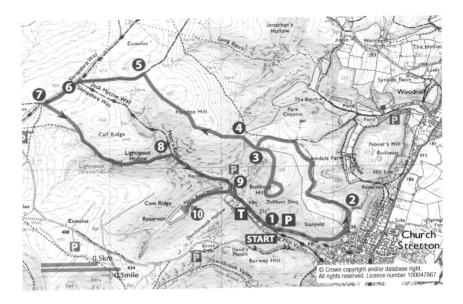

Walk directions

1 Follow the lane back towards Church Stretton. Just before the National Trust kiosk, fork left on a waymarked path that rises along the valley side. The path shortly swings across the shoulder of Stanyeld. Ignore a gate behind Church Stretton Golf Club and keep ahead beside beech trees. (The club, founded in 1898 is the oldest 18-hole course in the county and topping out at 375m is the third highest in the United Kingdom.) At the end, branch left on a track over a cattle grid.

2 Mindful of flying golf balls, resume the climb. After 800m, just beyond a second rise, look for a waypost. Again branch left, shortly passing a small hut and then a clump of trees. Nearing the edge of the course, swing left past a final green to a gate in the perimeter fence.

3 To reach Bodbury Ring, go left through a slight dip and then curve right on a rising trod towards its ramparts. Skirt the rim of the embanked defences, completing the circuit alongside a deep ditch and rampart that protected the 'neck' of the promontory fort. Swing right across the hillside back to the golf course gate (Point 3), but now remain on this side of the boundary, continuing past the gate.

4 Reaching the fence corner keep ahead to pick up a path that climbs steeply onto Haddon Hill. Cresting the top, walk on for 800m across heather moor. Eventually, the way fragments, but keep ahead with the main path to meet a broad gravel track.

5 Follow it left, later merging with Mott's Road, which has climbed out of the valley, and carry on to a junction.

6 Walk left with The Portway along the broad ridge of The Long Mynd for 400m to a prominent fork.

7 Leave the gravel track there, turning off sharp left on a grass path across the moor. Before long it begins to lose height towards the head of Lightspout Hollow. After dropping more steeply to cross a stream, swing right and follow the path down into the narrowing fold of the valley.

Lower down is the pretty waterfall of Light Spout. The path clambers past it on the left over a rocky outcrop before descending a steep flight of rough steps back to the stream at the base of the fall. Carry on beside the stream for another 400m to a junction at the foot of Lightspout Hollow.

Light Spout

8 Go right, crossing the stream to continue down the main valley to the top car park.

9 Just beyond the car park barrier, branch right over a footbridge on a path signed 'Reservoir'. Rising over a shoulder into New Pool Hollow, the path climbs up the side valley above the stream, passing small pools that held water for the carding mill. Reaching the foot of a high, steep grass bank, keep left to find steps beside it onto the top of the dam. The reservoir was completed 1902, the dam having taken three years to construct. It was built to replace a smaller, earlier dam in the Townbrook Valley, and provided piped water for the village until it was connected to the mains supply in 1977.

10 Return by the same route. Lower down you can branch right, remaining above the stream to cut the corner back to the main valley. Follow the lane to the right, soon bearing off left on a parallel path to bypass a ford. After a short distance the path crosses a bridge back to the lane. Walk on, passing the former mill and then the Chalet Pavilion to return to the main parking areas.

Walk 8 **Ashes Hollow and Pole Bank**

Deep, winding valleys and long, airy ridges connect Little Stretton with Pole Bank, the highest point of The Long Mynd

What to expect:
Generally good hill paths and tracks; long but steady ascent on the return

Distance/time: 10.5km/6½ miles. Allow 3½ to 4 hours
Start: Small car park by Pole Cottage on The Long Mynd
Grid ref: SO 412937
Ordnance Survey map: Explorer 217 (The Long Mynd & Wenlock Edge)
Refreshments: The Green Dragon and The Ragleth Inn in Little Stretton
Transport: None

Walk outline
Beginning along the broad ridge of Round Hill, there are fine views from the start across the head of Callow Hollow to Yapsel Bank. Dropping to the ancient earthwork of Cross Dyke, the route skirts the southern flank of Grindle. Crossing another saddle above the head of Small Batch, it then descends along the valley side into Little Stretton. The return rises gently along the secluded, meandering valley of Ashes Hollow, eventually climbing past the spring at its head onto the broad spine of The Long Mynd, then detouring over the ridge's high point back to the car park.

The Long Mynd

At 516m, Pole Bank is the highest point of The Long Mynd ridge and offers a fine panorama on a clear day. The topograph points optimistically out west to Cadair Idris, some 72km/45 miles away, but a much better bet for identification are the closer Shropshire hills. With a sea of heather stretching away in all directions, it is a grand spot, particularly in full summer when all is washed in a rich purple, no wonder it was reserved as the colour of Emperors.

The walk then wanders out onto the high ground of Round Hill, the contours progressively falling away ever more steeply into the deep, labyrinthine valleys on either side. Variously called hollows, batches and beaches, they are the result of fast-flowing meltwater streams cutting through the bedrock to meet the main Stretton valley, whose base had been ground down by the inexorable flow of a mighty glacier.

Descending to a narrow col below Round Hill, the path crosses through one of the several Bronze Age cross dykes to be found on these hills. Running for some 170m between the near precipitous slopes dropping away on either side of the ridge, the dyke, paralleled by a ditch below its western flank, separates Grindle Hill from the main body of the hill. Although not considered to be defensive, it nevertheless marked an ancient boundary. Higher up on a spur off Grindle Hill are two tumuli from the same period.

An attractive hamlet

The route drops off the hill into Little Stretton, an attractive hamlet with a couple of fine pubs and an unusual church. Despite its appearance, All Saints was only built in 1903, erected from a prefabricated kit supplied from Manchester. It was given to the village by Alice Elizabeth as a chapel of ease, following the death of her husband Rev John Gibbon six years earlier. Originally roofed in corrugated iron, services were interrupted by the noise of heavy rain and it was subsequently thatched, first with heather and then with reeds.

The walk climbs back onto the hill along the superbly beautiful valley of Ashes Hollow, following the tumbling stream to its source at the Boiling Well. The spring perhaps had some ancient significance, for just across the road to the north east is a low, heather-covered mound. Around 12m in diameter and originally surrounded by a ditch, it is a bowl barrow dating from the Bronze Age, some 4000 years ago. One of around 25 such tumuli scattered in prominent locations across The Long Mynd, it was built as a funerary monument and would have contained burials, usually of cremated remains, together with grave goods such as pottery, tools or personal artefacts.

Walk directions

1 Across the lane from the car park, a grass trod strikes away across the heather, shortly curving right towards the bulk of Round Hill. After 400m swing left along a broad, green path, which falls gently to a large grassy clearing. Ignoring the narrow path off left, keep ahead to a prominent fork and take the left branch, which rises over Round Hill. Descend beyond to the broad col of Barrister's Plain.

2 Pass through the ditch and rampart of Cross Dyke and curve right above Barrister's Batch. Skirting the southern slope of the hill, the path descends to another col connecting Grindle and Callow. Cross the saddle and slant down the steep north-eastern flank of Callow above Small Batch, eventually losing height through the pretty, wooded lower section of the valley. Walk out past a campsite, over a bridge beside a ford and swing right to a fork.

3 Both branches lead into the village, that on the right coming out by The Green Dragon, while the other meets the main road by The Ragleth Inn. Return past the fork towards the Small Batch campsite. Immediately after crossing the bridge beside the ford, leave over a stile on the right. Walk through the camping field to another stile at the top corner. Continue up the valley, shortly entering the National Trust's Long Mynd estate. Carry on, soon crossing the stream by a cottage.

4 Continue along the other bank. Farther on the fold narrows and the path becomes more rugged, occasionally crossing the stream to find the best route. However the way remains clear as it winds up the main gorge, passing the several tributary gullies that gather streams from the upper hill. Eventually, the valley opens out to the open moor of The Long Mynd ridge, the path rising to meet the lane near the Boiling Well, the spring source of the stream that falls through the valley.

5 Follow the lane briefly left before leaving along a broad track branching off right. Climb to a crossing of paths at the crest of the ridge and turn left to the top of Pole Bank, which is marked by a trig column and topograph.

6 Continue over the summit, descending towards the trees surrounding Pole Cottage. Meeting the lane, follow it right back to the car park.

Walk 9 **Caer Caradoc and Hope Bowdler Hill**

The legendary site of Caratacus's last stand against the imperial might of the Roman legions, Caer Caradoc is one of the finest viewpoints above Church Stretton

What to expect:
Generally good hill paths and tracks; two steep ascents onto the hills

Distance/time: 10.5km/6½ miles. Allow 3½ to 4 hours
Start: Lion Meadow car park in Church Stretton (pay and display)
Grid ref: SO 453936
Ordnance Survey map: Explorer 217 (The Long Mynd & Wenlock Edge)
Refreshments: Choice of pubs and cafés in Church Stretton
Transport: Rail and bus services to Church Stretton

Walk outline
Leaving the town, there is a leisurely climb into Cwms below Helmeth Hill before the ascent begins in earnest onto Caer Caradoc. After traversing the hilltop fort, the way descends south across an intervening saddle onto Hope Bowdler Hill. There is then another airy stretch along the ridge before descending steeply to Hazler. The return wanders back across sloping pastures before finally dropping to Church Stretton.

An ancient British hero

Caer Caradoc, the imposing hill to the north east of Church Stretton, is said by some to be the site of Caratacus's last stand against the Romans in AD51. The Romans had landed on British soil eight years earlier, and although some southern tribes submitted, Caratacus and his brother Togodumnus led the Catuvellauni tribe (centred on Colchester) in an ongoing guerrilla resistance. Despite some success, they were steadily pushed back and Togodumnus was killed at the River Thames. Retreating towards the Welsh hills, Caratacus fought on, enlisting the support of the Silures and then the Ordivices. But the Roman advance was relentless and Caratacus realised he had to gamble all on a decisive final battle. According to the Roman historian Tacitus, he chose his ground well, a high hill defended by steep sides and stone ramparts. At first the legions were repulsed, but then adopted testudo tactics, that is grouping close behind a wall of impenetrable shields to push forward through the defence. The battle was lost and Caratacus's family was taken, but he hid in a cave before escaping north to the Brigantes. However, their queen Cartimandua had given her allegiance to Rome and handed Caratacus over to the Roman general Ostorius Scapula. Taken to the imperial city, Caratacus was processed in chains during the general's victory parade, but before his execution, was allowed to address the Senate. His impassioned speech earned his release and he lived out his days with his family in Rome.

Church Stretton

Although overlooked by Iron Age forts from both the east and the west, and a major Roman road ran through the valley from Wroxeter to Leintwardine and on into South Wales, Church Stretton only emerged as a settlement during the Saxon period. The Domesday Book records a church, a relic of which appears in the form of a carved sheela-na-gig (squatting naked female figure) over the doorway of St Laurence's Church. The present building is from the 12th century, by which time the area was a royal manor overseen from a short-lived castle on Brockhurst Hill. Granted a charter in the 13th century, the town served the surrounding settlements throughout the Middle Ages. Although a disastrous fire in 1593 destroyed much of the town, it was soon rebuilt and many of today's half-timbered buildings date from that time.

By the 19th century, the town was becoming a haven for the wealthy and gentry, wishing to escape the grime and noise of urban industrialisation, and with its profusion of clear hillside springs, the town had ambitions of becoming a spa. Day trippers came with the arrival of the railway in 1852, and hotels and boarding houses sprang up to cater for longer term visitors. Although the spa came to nought, bank holiday crowds were modest and the valley became known as 'Little Switzerland'. But it was motor transport that changed everything. During summer weekends, the streets and the Carding Mill Valley became packed with charabancs and cars, and by 1938 the Council were imposing parking charges to cover the cost of cleaning up after hoards of picnickers. But the town learned to cope and tourism is now its main business, capitalising on the spectacular countryside. The outdoors is its greatest asset and Church Stretton led the way by becoming the first 'Walkers are Welcome' town in the Midlands.

The Gaer Stone

Walk directions

1 From the bottom of the car park walk left. At the end, turn right along Sandford Avenue, branching left past the fire and police stations and then left again into Essex Road. Keep ahead at the bend for another 200m, passing Windsor Place before taking a footapth off on the right. Carefully cross the railway and head at the edge of a paddock to the main road.

2 Cross to a kissing gate opposite and continue over another paddock, swinging left below a bank to find a kissing gate in the corner. Go right to a second gate, cross a track to another gate and walk up beside a small housing estate. Passing out at the top, curve right in the corner of a field to emerge through a gate onto Cwms Lane.

Go left for 100m, leaving immediately before a cattle grid through a gate on the right. Walk up the field above a sunken track, swinging left within the corner. Leave at the top along a hedged track, which rises through a wooded fold between Helmeth Hill and Caer Caradoc.

3 At the crest, fork left onto a narrow path over a plank bridge. After some 50m, go left again. Climb steeply away, passing through a gate to carry on up the snout of the hill. Beyond Three Fingers Rock, the gradient eases over intermediate summits towards the southern ramparts of the Caradoc fort straddling the high point.

4 Continue beyond, dropping steeply from the northern defences and over Little Caradoc, which then comes into view. As the gradient lessens, a fence joins from the right. Follow it briefly down to a gate.

5 Through it, a grass track curves back across the hill's eastern flank. Beyond a gate and over a rise make for a gate at the bottom.

6 Emerging onto a track follow it right. After 250m, immediately beyond a clump of tall pine, swing off left. Follow a trod around the side of a low hill, veering gently right to a gate in the far hedge. Bear left, climbing through bracken towards the saddle of the hill. Reaching the crest, go right and tackle the final pull onto the summit of Hope Bowdler Hill.

7 Walk on along the ridge to the second top, which, although lower, has a larger cairn and arguably better view to Caer Caradoc. Beyond, the path runs past a small outcrop marking the end of the ridge before dropping to the Gaer Stone and a kissing gate. Instead of going through, turn right and follow a fence steeply down. Leaving the access land, continue downfield to a track. Follow it left towards the road.

8 Just before the end, go through a gate on the right to follow a permissive path above the road. Continue at the left edge of a field, swinging within its corner to a kissing gate. Go right at the top edge of the next field. In the corner, ignore the stile and swing left downhill. Towards the bottom, bypass the hedged garden of a house to leave over a stile onto a narrow lane. Turn left and retrace your outward route back into town.

Walk 10 **Ragleth Hill and Acton Scott**

Surrounded by impressive-looking hills, Church Stretton is the focus for many appealing walks, this one looping out over Ragleth Hill to the Historic Working Farm at Acton Scott.

What to expect:
Field paths and quiet lanes; steep pull to start the walk from the town

Distance/time: 11.7km/7½ miles. Allow 4 to 4½ hours
Start: Lion Meadow car park in Church Stretton (pay and display)
Grid ref: SO 453936
Ordnance Survey map: Explorer 217 (The Long Mynd & Wenlock Edge)
Refreshments: Choice of pubs and cafés in Church Stretton, café at Acton Scott's Historic Working Farm (visitors only)
Transport: Rail and bus services to Church Stretton

Walk outline
Leaving the town, the walk climbs the steep northern flanks of Ragleth Hill, getting the day's major ascent out of the way at the start. Then follows a splendid trek along the hill's broad ridge before dropping to the quiet lanes. Acton Scott working farm is just a short distance from the route. The return across fields and on quiet lanes, finally descends through a wooded fold back to the town.

An impressive view

Although lower than neighbouring Caer Caradoc, the ascent of Ragleth
Hill still demands an energetic pull and the panorama across the Stretton
Gap to the deep hollows and batches cleaving The Long Mynd is equally
impressive. Once on the ridge, there is a wonderful airy walk before
dropping gently across the rolling countryside behind to Acton Scott.

Acton Scott and an historic farm

Acton Scott rose to fame during 2009, when it featured in the BBC
Television's six-part Victorian Farm series, but its farming origins can be
traced back to Iron Age field enclosures. A Roman villa was discovered
to the east of the present farm and on the eve of the Norman Conquest
the manor was one of many held by the Saxon thegn, Eadric Silvaticus.
Known as Eadric the Wild, he was one of the richest and most powerful
men in the region.

Following the invasion, William began to establish his position, and
required the Saxon nobles to submit to his rule. But Eadric refused
and, garnering support from the Welsh, led a rebellion against the new

overlords. He first attacked Hereford, but was unable to take the castle and retreated to regroup with a force from Cheshire. He then turned his attentions to Shrewsbury, burning the town, but again failing to capture the castle. After losing a decisive battle at Stratford, he realised the futility of his cause and finally submitted. William confiscated a large portion of his holdings, nevertheless Eadric fell in with the king as he headed north to invade Scotland.

Eadric's capitulation was seen by some as treachery and legend has it that he was imprisoned in the Stiperstones lead mines. It is said that when the country's freedom is threatened, he appears with his fairy wife Godda, leading a band of warriors to confront the danger.

Today, the manor is held by the Actons, who can trace their ancestry here all the way back to the 13th century. But by the time Thomas Acton took over the estate in the 1960s, farming was undergoing a major revolution and he realised that, without action, many traditional farming practices of previous generations would soon be forgotten. His vision created the Acton Scott Historic Working Farm, which is centred upon the 18th-century Home Farm. Using traditional machinery, skills and rare breed species, the farm is a working museum and practical demonstration of 19th-century farming life.

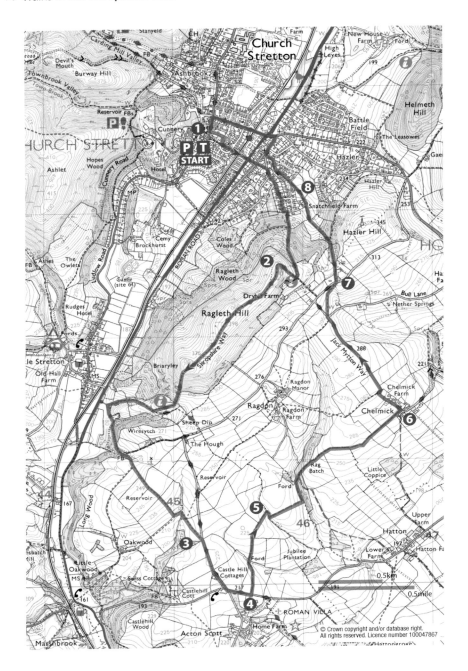

Walk directions

1 From the bottom of the car park walk left. At the end, go right along Sandford Avenue, branching right to the railway. The railway came to Church Stretton in 1852, enabling the town's emergence as a holiday and day visitor destination. However, the original station lay just to the north, on the other side of the road bridge, its buildings still standing but no longer used by the railway. Use the station footbridge to cross the line and walk out to the main road. Take the street opposite, proceeding over the next junction into Clive Avenue. Follow it on up the hill, keeping ahead onto Ragleth Road and eventually turning right into Poplar Drive.

The Shropshire Way continues between houses at the end. Over stiles, wind left and then right to climb steeply through coppice. Keep going beyond another stile, the path shortly breaking onto the shoulder of the hill. Swing sharp right in front of a gate to tackle the final pull to the top.

2 The ongoing path undulates along the crest, giving grand views to The Long Mynd's batches. Pause on the third top, marked by a tall pole, to enjoy the view before dropping determinedly to the corner of a fence. Continue downhill with the fence on your left to a stile. Bear left across bracken to another stile and walk on to the far-left corner of the next pasture. Head down to emerge at the bottom of the left hedge onto a narrow lane.

3 Go right, following the lane around a left bend. Carry on for 1.2km to reach a cross-roads. Turn left towards Ticklerton and Acton Scott Farm, walking past the village hall to a drive leading to Acton Scott Bed and Breakfast.

4 The open-air museum of Acton Scott Farm, which also has an excellent café, lies just a little further along the lane and is well worth a visit if time allows. However, the way back to Church Stretton is through a gateway on the left opposite the B&B drive. Follow a tractor track to a gate in the far-left field corner. Swing right to a second gate and climb away, initially along

a sunken path before vegetation forces you onto the field edge.
The hedged path later reappears, descending to a gate and stream.

5 Climb right, swinging within the field corner. Over the rise, go left
again at the next corner, walking on to a gate. Through that, bend right,
crossing a stream to the edge of a wood. Ignore a gate on the right and
climb through the trees to a gate at the top. Keep going at the field
edge, finally leaving along a hedged track that leads out to a narrow lane
opposite Chelmick Farm.

6 Follow the lane uphill for 800m, abandoning it just past a junction
through a kissing gate on the right. Head out across grazing to find a stile
in the far corner onto another lane.

7 Take the track opposite to Church Stretton, which drops across the slope
of a wooded fold. After crossing a stream, emerge into a field and carry on
downhill. Joining a fence, pass between the old buildings of Snatchfield
Farm and continue along a track, which ends at the edge of housing.

Keep ahead on a footpath leading to another street, which at the bottom
meets Clive Avenue. Retrace your outward steps into the town.

Walk 11 **Bishop's Castle and Oakeley Mynd**

An attractive border market town and fine views across rolling hills make this a walk to savour

What to expect:
Mainly field paths and tracks; steady ascents that are not unduly steep

Distance/time: 12.5km/7¾ miles. Allow 4 to 4½ hours
Start: Auction Yard car park on Church Street, (not on stock market days)
Grid ref: SO 324886
Ordnance Survey map: Explorer 216 (Welshpool & Montgomery)
Refreshments: Choice of pubs and cafés in Bishop's Castle, Powis Arms at Lydbury North
Transport: Bishop's Castle is served by a bus service from Shrewsbury

Walk outline
Leaving the town past its church, the walk heads to the foot of Oakeley Mynd, briefly following a lane before rising over its southern shoulder to the neighbouring village of Lydbury North. There is a pub for refreshment and a church to explore before climbing out across the fields towards Totterton. The return is around the northern flank of the hill, dropping through woodland back to Oakeley Farm and then retracing your steps back to town.

A frontier town

Bishop's Castle has been a market town since AD102 when it was granted a charter by King John. Since the 9th century, the manor had been held by the Bishops of Hereford, a generous gift of the wealthy Saxon landowner Egwin Shakehead in thanks for the miraculous cure of his shaking palsy at the shrine of St Ethelburt in Hereford. For the next 250 years, the settlement was probably no more than a few farms and houses clustered around the church. However, as the Normans extended their advance into Wales, they appointed the Bishops of Hereford as Marcher Lords to consolidate their rule across the border lands. Hard against the Welsh border, the manor was vulnerable to attack and, around 1085, a castle was established on the high ground – the Bishop's Castle.

Originally a simple motte and bailey, it was later extended and a new 'plantation' town laid out in burgage plots down the hill towards the church. The grants of land were designed to attract 'settlers' bringing stability, prosperity and trade and carried the privileges of burgess, rights to be free men holding land and property. The ancient grid pattern of parallel streets and interconnecting alleys remain. Despite the periodic unrest of a border post, the town prospered through the Middle Ages, based around a trade in livestock being driven from Wales along the ancient Kerry Ridgeway to English markets.

A charter from Elizabeth I in 1584 allowed the town to elect two burgesses to Parliament, a practice that continued through the centuries. But with so few freemen entitled to vote, it developed into a 'rotten borough', where bribery could effectively buy a seat in Parliament. The practice ended with the 1832 Reform

Act and Bishop's Castle was disenfranchised, to be absorbed within a wider constituency. However, one man is celebrated as refusing bribes, the 'honest burgess' Matthew Marston, who died in 1802. His gravestone can be found in the churchyard.

Over time, the castle became ruinous, its stones finding their way into the town's later buildings. At the beginning of the 18th century, much of the site was cleared to make way for a bowling green and only fragments of the walls remain. But wandering around Bishop's Castle you will discover a wealth of other fine buildings, including the Old Porch House, the Old Hall and the House on Crutches, now a museum. The town has several worthy inns, but the Three Tuns is the oldest, dating back to at least 1642. Until recently, it had always brewed its own ale – the brewhouse standing next door, and although the two are now run as separate enterprises, the close link continues. The Castle Hotel was built on the site of the castle in 1719 and was for a time owned by Robert Clive – Clive of India, whose family held considerable land in the area. The church stands at the opposite end of the town to the castle, rebuilt after it was destroyed by Parliamentarians during the Civil War. There are several interesting headstones in the graveyard.

Lydbury North

The church to St Michael and All Angels at Lydbury North is also worth a visit. It contains carved pews and a fine pulpit, while beautifully lettered above the entrance to the chancel, are the Articles of Faith, the Ten Commandments and the Lord's Prayer. Unusually, the Plowden Chapel, still owned by the family is a Roman Catholic chapel, with masses occasionally said, and above the Walcot Chapel is the old school, which was in use as such from 1662 until 1843.

Along the walk, keep a lookout for red kites. At one time a common sight, they stopped nesting in the area after 1876 and by the 1930s were virtually extinct. However, successful breeding pairs have been recorded since 2006 and glimpses of these graceful fliers are becoming more common.

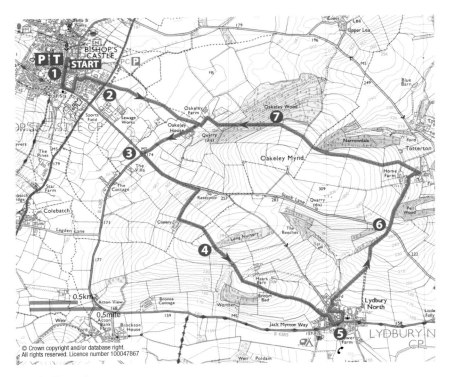

Walk directions

1 Walk west through the car park and along an alley to emerge on Church Street beside the King's Head. Go left, over a junction and then swing left in front of the church. After 100m, leave along a footpath on the left behind houses. Partway along, turn right into the estate and follow the street left. Continue on a path beyond its end onto a drive. Through a kissing gate on the left, another path leads to the main road.

2 Over a stile opposite, strike across the town's show field to a stile halfway along the far hedge. Cross the next field to a stile in its indented corner and keep going over two more fields, aiming just right of Oakeley Farm. Exit through a clump of trees onto a track and go right to a road junction.

3 Turn left uphill. After 500m, leave through a signposted gate on the right. Walk left along the field edge to a concrete track and follow it right to the farmyard at Conery. There, swing left through a gate and continue up beside a field. Over a stile, carry on, passing right of a woodland strip across the crest, the Long Nursery.

4 Through a succession of gates, keep going at the field edge, skirting above a deep valley and down to a green barn. Through a gate to its right, remain by the left boundary. Over a stile in the corner, a hollow way leads on down the hill, abruptly ending onto a street. Walk to the bottom and turn right to the main road, where the Powis Arms lies a short distance to the right.

5 The route, however, is to the left. Just beyond the church, go left again up a lane. At the end go right and then swing left past Bridleway Cottage. Climb away along another old track. At the top, ignore the path off left and continue a few metres farther to break out along the edge of a field. Carry on at the perimeter of more fields to the edge of a wood. Swing right beside it, departing through a gate at the top onto a junction of lanes.

6 Take the narrow lane opposite, eventually winding around a bend. As you then approach a black and white cottage, leave over a stile on the left. Climb to the edge of a field and strike out to a stile in the far hedge. Over a farm track, maintain the same direction uphill from field to field, passing a wood over to the right. The way then begins to lose height, dropping across the corner of a third field towards more woodland.

7 Look for a stile near a couple of dead trees into the plantation, from which a path angles down left. Ignoring a crossing track, carry on down to leave the trees through a gate. Continue across an open slope towards another gate at the bottom, swinging right in front of it. Follow the left hedge towards Oakeley Farm. Exit over a couple of stiles onto a track and go left. Almost immediately the track bends right and then left, at which point, watch for a fingerpost marking a path through the trees on the right. Breaking into a large field, head out to retrace your outward path back to town.

Walk 12 **Clun and Bury Ditches**

Over the hills to picturesque Clun and its castle, returning past one of the area's most impressive hilltop forts

What to expect:
Good field paths and woodland tracks, with a stretch along a lane, steady climbs

Distance/time: 13.7km/8½ miles. Allow 4½ to 5 hours
Start: Bury Ditches car park, off minor lane 3.2km/2 miles N of Clunton
Grid ref: SO 333839
Ordnance Survey map: Explorer
Refreshments: The Sun and White Horse inns, together with The Maltings Café at Clun; Tea on the Way at Guilden Down
Transport: None

Walk outline
The route begins along the southern flank of Sunnyhill, winding in above a narrow, wooded valley before breaking out to contour open fields below Steppleknoll. After skirting the edge of Radnor Wood, there is a long, gentle descent into Clun. After wandering around the picturesque town, the way back joins the Shropshire Way across the fields to the hills, climbing the forested slopes to the summit of Sunnyhill to see the spectacular Bury Ditches fort.

Saxon origins and a border castle

Straddling the river from which it took its name, Clun began as a 7th-century Saxon settlement clustered around its church on the southern side of the river. However, with the arrival of the Normans some 300 years later, it was granted to Picot de Say, one of the powerful Marcher Lords. Empowered to defend the unsettled border with Wales, he chose a bluff overlooking the river's opposite bank on which to establish a castle. Later refortified in stone, the castle became a strategic centre for border defence, drawing service from both local knights and the Welsh villages under its protection. As at Bishop's Castle (Walk 17), the Normans established a new town to encourage settlement and, despite its front-line position, Clun prospered from livestock and wool trades as a market town.

During the 12th century, ownership of the Barony had passed to the FitzAlans, who subsequently fell out with the king over questions of inheritance and loyalty. This was at a time of Welsh uprisings, and the King asserted his position by taking the town and garrisoning the castle with royal troops. But, with the relative peace that followed Edward I's conquest of Wales, and the subsequent move of the FitzAlans to their new seat at Arundel towards the end of the 13th century, the castle's importance declined and it became little more than a manor court and hunting lodge for the estate. Nevertheless, the castle saw action for a final time during the Owain Glyndŵr's rebellion at the start of the 15th century, but thereafter fell into disuse.

The ruins are dominated by a massive four-storey keep, which overlooks the inner bailey. Built by the FitzAlans in the early 13th century, it was as much a statement of power and wealth as defence. Together with the earthwork fortifications, a couple of turret towers and sections of the curtain wall, it remains an impressive sight. As a garrisoned castle, the walls would have enclosed various buildings such as a great hall, chapel and lodging for soldiers and servants, as well as kitchens, stores and stables. On the far riverbank are earthworks of a medieval pleasure garden, which included fishponds, dovecote and orchard - a pleasant escape for the court as well as providing food for the table.

One of the quietest places under the sun

Retaining its Norman grid pattern, Clun is a picturesque town and the smallest in Shropshire, still deserving of Housman's description as 'one of the quietest places under the sun'. He perhaps did not visit in May, when the springtime festival is centred upon a battle between the Green Man and the Frost Queen to allow summer into the town. Among the sites are the attractive 17th-century Trinity Hospital almshouses, which were founded by Henry Howard, Earl of Northampton. The six cottages and a chapel were built around a secluded courtyard to provide charitable accommodation for 12 poor men of good character. They still serve as retired accommodation (although married couples are now accepted too), and, while the cottages themselves are obviously private, the chapel can be visited. In the market square, the Buffalo Inn is reputedly where, inspired by the castle ruins, Sir Walter Scott wrote his novel 'The Betrothed', while farther along is the Town Hall, built by Edward, son of Robert Clive (of India) in 1780 to replace a medieval building; it is now a museum. Some of Clun's oldest dwellings lie over the medieval packhorse bridge, lining the street up to St George's Church. They once housed several craftsmen and a handful of pubs. The earliest parts of the church are Norman, the arches and columns lining

Almshouses

the nave and the lower stages of the tower. However, its raised, circular graveyard and an ancient yew, reputed to be over 2,000 years old, point to the site having a religious significance even predating the previous Saxon church. Amongst the gravestones are memorials to the playwright John Osborne, known for his play 'Look Back in Anger', and his last wife Helen, who lived in nearby Clunton, and a sad memorial to seven siblings who died at a young age of a 'putrid fever' within a short period during 1811.

An Iron Age settlement

Bury Ditches on Sunnyhill is one Britain's best preserved hillforts. Dating from around 500 BC, it is defended by multiple ramparts and ditches with complex entrances at either end that exposed potential invaders to concerted attack. Its construction represents a formidable achievement in planning, clearance and construction, which would have been undertaken using only simple axes and picks. Such places were not purely defensive and evidence from excavations suggests a permanent settlement of some size. Its positioning would certainly have made an impressive statement of tribal power. The view from the high point is extensive, stretching to Snowdon, more than 95km/60 miles away.

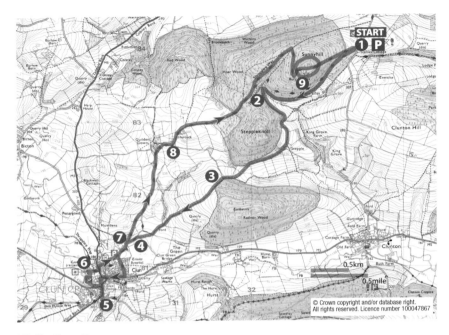

Walk directions

1 Follow a broad track beyond the car park, which contours the southern flank of Sunnyhill. After some 470m, at a waymarked fork by a bench, branch off left on a lower path. It later climbs to curve around the head of a valley before joining a track from the right.

2 Continue down, later leaving just before a bend through a kissing gate on the left. Turn right, initially below the trees, then bearing down to join a track. Walk on through a gate to Steeple Farm, forking right through the farmyard. Carry on, branching right on a green track. After 300m, at a waypost immediately beyond a gate, bear half-left across a field to a plank bridge. Maintain the line up to a gate in the corner. Carry on in the next field, swinging left at the top to a bridle gate into trees. The path climbs on at the forest edge, soon joining another path to a gate.

3 Stick by the hedge over the crest, the way later intermittently contained. Eventually, beyond a footbridge, the track widens to a sharp bend. Leave over a stile and bear right to a footbridge just left of the far corner.

4 Emerging onto a lane, go left towards Clun. At a junction beyond the Memorial Hall, fork left onto Hospital Lane, shortly passing an iron gateway, behind which old almshouses and a chapel are set within a garden. At the bottom of the lane, turn right along High Street past the 16th-century Sun Inn and into The Square, where the old town hall houses the town's museum. At the far end, keep ahead and then go left down Buffalo Lane. At the bottom, walk on over a narrow bridge spanning the River Clun. To find St George's Church, carry on up the hill.

5 From the church, retrace your steps, going left just before the bridge to a riverside car park, from which a path leaves beside the toilets to a footbridge over the river. Walk forward and then rake back up the banking, going left at the top to the castle.

6 Leaving the castle site, head east past the blowling green to the main road. Go left and then right between buildings along a footpath that leads to the Memorial Hall and car park (alternative start). Continue through to the road and go left, passing YHA hostel (once the town's mill, still containing the original machinery).

7 At the next bend, fork left before a small garage with the Shropshire Way on a rising track. A contained path skirts Mill House to a stile. Strike half-left across fields to regain the lane. Continue uphill for 800m, keeping right through a farm at Guilden Down.

8 Immediately past a cottage and tea garden, fork left to the top of the hill. There, branch right past a barrier into forest. Through a gate, keep ahead, before long joining a broad track from the left. Ignore side tracks, but keep left with the Shropshire Way at a fork to climb above a valley. Passing a path off right, continue to the crest and go right with the Shropshire Way. Contour around to a gate from which a path rises to the western entrance of the hilltop fort.

9 Paths run through the middle and either side along the still-formidable embankments, the one on the left passing a topograph on the high point. After exploring the ramparts, leave on a path dropping from the eastern entrance. Pass through a gate and keep going downhill to the car park.

Walk 13 **Black Hill**

A forest walk overlooking the Clun valley, with fine views from the top of the hill

What to expect:
Generally good forest paths and tracks; steady ascent to the top of the hill

Distance/time: 11.7km/7¼ miles. Allow 4 to 4½ hours
Start: Small Forest car park off minor lane south of Clunton
Grid ref: SO 337806
Ordnance Survey map: Explorer 201 (Knighton & Presteigne)
Refreshments: The Crown Inn, Clunton
Transport: Local bus service through Clunton

Walk outline
Starting from a roadside car park above Clunton, the route contours across the flanks of Sowdley Wood before winding up the forested north western slopes of Black Hill. After deviating from a minor top for the view, the way continues more easily in a circuit of the main summit. The return makes a steady descent along the side of a steep valley before cutting back through the thick of the trees to the car park.

Inspiration from the hills

Not every walk need have a finite goal, a must-reach summit or outstanding feature for which to aim. The purpose of the day can simply be the pleasure of an enjoyable walk in the countryside, the exercise of the body and the relaxation of the mind. And this is just such a walk; demanding some exertion in a quiet corner of the county where you're not going to meet too many people. Some aspects have not changed since the late 19th century when the poet A. E. Housman wrote:

'Clunton and Clunbury,
Clungunford and Clun,
Are the quietest places
Under the sun'

The novelist and travel writer, Bruce Chatwin also gained inspiration from this unfrequented corner of border country. During a stay with friends at nearby Cwm Hall, he penned the beginning of his famous novel On the Black Hill, which was awarded the James Tait Black Memorial Prize and subsequently made into a film. Black Hill overlooks Clunton, set in the valley of the River Clun, a tranquil hamlet straddling a minor road and worth a visit in the evening or at weekend for its pub, if nothing else.

At 441m, the summit of Black Hill just peaks above its near neighbours. However, for some reason it appears to have been ignored by Celtic chieftains, for there is no earthwork, fort or cairn on its top, unlike Sunnyhill just across the valley, which is the site of the impressive Bury Ditches.

A working forest

Nevertheless, it is a fair-sized hill, flanked on all but its western aspect by steep slopes that fall into deep valleys. These days, like many of its neighbours, it has been planted as commercial forest, but hidden amongst the trees you will come across occasional old boundaries and gateposts, relics of an earlier age when the hillsides were divided up as grazing meadows. A modern artefact is a communications mast, although it is not sited on the high point. The summit is crowned by the customary trig column, but for the time being, is barely accessible, surrounded by an almost impenetrable growth of trees.

Yet, as with any forested area, nothing is static. Seedling conifers are planted thickly and one or two cycles of thinning are often necessary during the growth cycle. When the plot reaches maturity, clear-felling takes place, opening up areas from which there may have been no view for years. The bare brash left behind might look unsightly at first, but is quickly colonised as dormant plants and windblown seeds take advantage of the newly created space. Foxgloves and rosebay willowherb are often among the first to appear, but look closely and you'll find many smaller flowers sprouting through as well. The brash also helps protect the soil from the heavy plant and machinery during the felling process and, as it decomposes, puts fertility back into the land for a new generation of planting.

An ancient woodland

If you have time to spare after the walk, head just a little farther up the hill from the car park to find the entrance to Clunton Coppice. Managed by Shropshire Wildlife Trust, it is celebrated as a 'Wood for all Seasons'. Although dominated by sessile oak, which was once managed for charcoal, the woodland is well scattered with birch, holly, hazel and yew, which together provide foliage colour throughout the year. In spring, the open canopy allows a proliferation of wildflowers such as wood anemone, while in autumn an amazing variety of fungi sprouts up amongst the leaf litter. There are birds aplenty too, listen out for great spotted woodpeckers and watch for wood warblers and pied flycatchers in summer.

Pied flycatcher

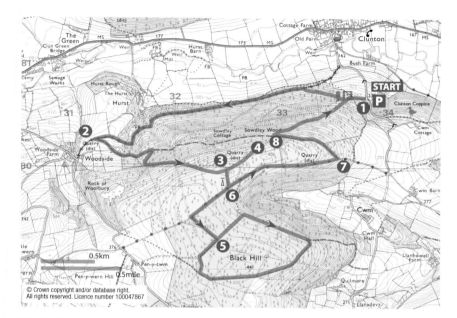

Walk directions

1 Leave along a barriered track from the rear right corner of the car park, which rises above the Clun valley. Shortly, at a crossing, turn right down to meet a lower track from Clunton. To the left, it undulates easily within the bottom of the forest. Eventually, after winding around a couple of side valleys, the track breaks from the trees. Meeting the bend of a farm track, keep ahead to a junction.

2 Double back left, climbing past Pooh Hall Cottages to re-enter the forest past a barrier. After 400m, look for a waymarked track leaving sharp right. Follow it up, branching left at a fork to a junction and go left again. Continue the steady plod up the hill, keeping ahead at two more junctions. As the gradient then starts to ease, the track breaks from the trees by a transmitter mast on the broad summit ridge.

3 First, walk forward for the view as the ground begins to fall away. To the north is Sunnyhill, the embankments of Bury Ditches clearly visible, while farther round is The Long Mynd and hills around Church Stretton.

4 Retrace your steps to the transmitter and go left past a barrier following the margin between forest plots. Swing right with the main track past a junction (Point 6) and walk on for some 500m. Reaching another junction at the crest of the hill, turn left and continue between the different plantations to a T-junction.

5 Turn right, shortly curving around to a junction. Keep left and continue around Black Hill. Beyond a gentle rise the path curves left to be joined by another from the right. The way now starts to fall, eventually bending left again. Keep ahead as another path then enters from the right to contour above a steep, wooded slope. Eventually the track bends left again, now climbing to return to Point 5. Go right, reversing your outward steps and turning right again to the junction at Point 6.

6 This time, instead of turning left to the transmitter, keep ahead on an initially rough grass track. Gently losing height, the track later breaks out at the edge of the forest to run beside a high deer fence.

7 Reaching the second high gate through the deer fence on your right, look for a metal field gate set back on the left. Marked as a bridleway, a track rises away. Beyond a shallow crest, the track splits. Take the downward right branch to another junction.

8 There go sharp right on a descending broad track. Keep ahead at a crossing lower down to return to the car park.

Walk 14 **Knighton and Offa's Dyke**

A ramble from the border town of Knighton along a striking section of
Offa's Dyke and returning by a roundabout route across the hills on
the English side

What to expect:
Generally clear field and woodland paths; a steep ascent leaving the town.

Distance/time: 13.3km/8¼ miles. Allow 4½ to 5 hours
Start: Bowling Green car park (pay and display), south of A488 towards
eastern edge of Knighton
Grid ref: SO 288722
Ordnance Survey map: Explorer 201 (Knighton & Presteigne)
Refreshments: Choice of pubs and cafés in Knighton
Transport: Knighton is served by both bus and rail services

Walk outline
*Following Offa's Dyke, the walk climbs steeply from Knighton above the
Teme valley. Turning from the old border into England, the way falls across
fields to Five Turnings. Another steady pull leads onto the Stow Hill plateau,
the path then turning down an impressive gully past Holloway Rocks to the
hamlet of Stowe. After a stretch through fields, the final leg contours the
lower slopes of Kinsley Wood back to town.*

Offa's Dyke

Since Henry VIII's Laws in Wales Act of 1535, Knighton has been in Wales, but only just, for the border here winds east-west with the River Teme running at its foot. The original border traditionally defined by Offa, the 8th-century king of Mercia, ran north-south favouring the high ground, but dipping to cross the river at what would become Knighton. There is no record of there being an Anglo-Saxon town at this spot, although it is likely and its Welsh name of Tref-y-Clawdd does mean Town of the Dyke. Offa ruled his kingdom for almost 40 years until AD796, a vast land that reached back from Wales to the Lincolnshire Fens and stretched from beyond the River Mersey down to the Thames valley. The imposing dyke establishing the frontier with the Welsh kingdoms ran intermittently for 240km/150 miles between Chester and Chepstow, and was carefully sited to give clear views into Wales. It is not known whether it served as a functioning defence or merely an imposing symbol of power, but whatever, some 20m wide at its base and rising around 8m above a deep ditch, it would have presented an intimidating sight. Recent research suggests some sections of the dyke might have been constructed before the traditionally accepted dates and thus the result of a longer term undertaking by successive monarchs. The short section of the dyke followed during this walk is as impressive as any along the whole of the Offa's Dyke long distance path.

A Norman border town

By the time of William's Domesday Survey, there was an established settlement held by the unflatteringly named Hugh the Ass. Under the Normans it became a strategic border and later market town protected by a castle. It is thought the original motte stood in the centre of the town, with Bryn y Castell, another earthwork just to the east, being built after the town was sacked in 1262 by Llywelyn ap Gruffudd. The town was overrun again at the beginning of the 15th century during Owain Glyndŵr's revolt against the English crown. The English under Edmund Mortimer, younger son of the 3rd Earl of March, retreated south over the hill before being overwhelmed at Pilleth. Mortimer was captured, but when the King refused to pay ransom for him, Mortimer formed an alliance with Glyndŵr, married the rebel's daughter and put forward his nephew's claim to the English throne. In the end Glyndŵr's rebellion came to nought, Mortimer dying of exhaustion while besieged at Harlech Castle in 1409.

Prosperous years

With the end of conflict across the Marches, Knighton prospered and by the 18th and 19th centuries had become an important centre of the wool trade. The arrival of the railway from Craven Arms in 1861 brought a further boost to the town, but its construction had been a troubled undertaking with delays caused by poor weather and financial difficulties. The line subsequently continued through the sparsely populated valleys of central Wales, and although the potential for local traffic was limited, the main intention was to connect the coal and iron of South Wales with the major industrial centres in the Midlands and north. The station was not built until four years later, curiously standing across the river in England, but provided a speedy outlet for the town's livestock and wool markets. The line remains in use today, a scenic journey winding through the heart of Wales.

Exploring the town

The town's two castles survive only as earth mounds, neither having been built in stone. Bryn y Castell is a public park, but the other lies within a private garden. The town's Norman roots may be more readily apparent in its church. It has been suggested that the original foundation around the end of the 10th century, replaced by a Norman building some time during the middle of the 12th century, may have been a chapel of ease to nearby Stowe, passed on the return leg of the walk. Although the tower looks distinctly medieval, only the lower stage of the tower is 14th century, the rest being the result of a Victorian restoration, which superseded an early rebuilding in Georgian style in 1752, when it was dedicated to St Lawrence. Its present dedication is to Edward the Confessor, who was canonised in 1161 and regarded as England's patron saint until the adoption of St George around 1350. The Gothic clock tower, which was erected in 1872, stands on the spot where a man could obtain a divorce by auctioning his wife. The last recorded sale occurred in 1854, with the husband receiving the princely sum of one shilling (5p).

River Teme

The walk begins along the banks of the River Teme, which has its source in the Kerry Hills, south of Newtown in Powys. At Knighton it crosses the border into England and then winds its way through Shropshire and Worcestershire before it enters the Severn to the south of Worcester. The river was designated an SSSI in 1996 and in its upper reaches are to be found rare freshwater pearl-mussel and native white clawed crayfish. As you pass by, watch out for brown trout, dipper and sand martin.

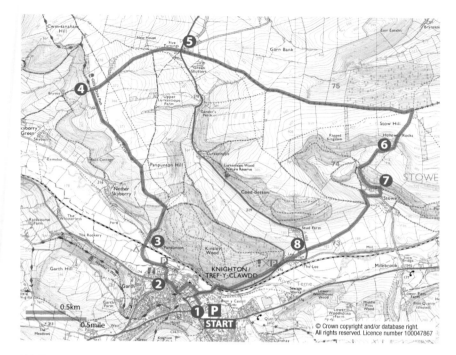

Walk directions

1 Turn right from the car park along Bowling Green Lane to the main road. Go right and first left along Church Road. Passing St Edward's Church, swing left to the town centre. Emerging opposite the clock tower, head right to the Offa's Dyke information centre.

2 Turn down beside it and follow Offa's Dyke signs on a path across the grass. Fork left past a skate park and then branch right down steps to a riverside path. Go left, passing a bridge straddling the boundary between England and Wales. Carry on beside the Teme to a footbridge, over which, carefully cross a railway line. Continue briefly upstream before swinging right at the fence corner to emerge beside a stable onto a lane.

3 Through another gate opposite, take the right-hand path. Climb through trees beside Offa's Dyke to a fingerpost. Fork left and head steeply up a bracken-covered hillside. At the top, go left, rising more easily past a wood and follow the dyke across the undulating slopes of the upper hill. Keep going through occasional gates and past a picturesque stand of pine, eventually reaching a gate and crossing track.

4 Turn right over the crest, continuing past a small plantation. Strike across the subsequent field, descending to a gate at the distant corner. A broad track leads out to a junction of roads at Five Turnings.

5 Take the track opposite to Five Turnings Farm. Go past the house along a gently climbing track, eventually reaching a conifer plantation. Keep ahead beside the trees. Approaching the far end of the second field, turn off right. Pass a small pool on your left and head over the crest, curving gently right to a fence gate, shortly becoming visible.

6 A stone track drops steeply through a deep cleft in the scar of Holloway Rocks. At a fork, swing right, the gradient easing to pass a pond. Through a gate lower down, continue into woodland, keeping with the main track to a country church.

7 There fork right, winding down to another junction. Turn right, not over the cattle grid, but along a gravel track that falls to a bridge spanning a stream. Carry on over a cattle grid, re-crossing the stream towards a house. Through a gate on the left, drop across the stream and go left, rising back across the hillside to a bridle gate. Through that, turn up beside the fence to the top corner. Ignoring crossing tracks, walk ahead through the leftmost of three gates and stride on, gently descending beside the left hedge. Walk from field to field, the hedge eventually on your right, finally reaching the main road.

8 Cross diagonally left to a stile and head out over a field, crossing an intervening footbridge to find a stile in the far corner below Kinsley Wood. Climb steps to the bend of a gravel track and follow it briefly downhill, leaving just before a forestry sign for a path off right. Ultimately descending to the road, cross to the opposite footway and carry on into town. Stay with the main road over the railway, shortly turning left along Bowling Green Lane back to the car park.

Walk 15 **Bucknell Hill**

Forest and open hills on this ramble around the pretty Redlake valley above Bucknell

What to expect:
Generally good paths and tracks; sustained but not unduly steep ascents

Distance/time: 12.5km/7¾ miles. Allow 4½ to 5 hours
Start: Roadside parking in Bucknell or Hopton Wood forest car park (minor lane 2.5km/1½ miles west of Bedstone, alternative start)
Grid ref: SO 354738/SO 345762
Ordnance Survey map: Explorer 201 (Knighton & Presteigne)
Refreshments: Sitwell Arms and The Baron at Bucknell
Transport: Bus and rail services to Bucknell

Walk outline
From the church, the walk leaves Bucknell to climb through the conifer plantations of Bucknell Wood onto a spur of Stow Hill. A long descent back into the Redlake valley is followed by an initially steep pull up on the other side of the vale onto Bedstone Hill. Back in trees, the way dips across a broad col onto Bucknell Hill before winding down across more open farmland back to the village.

An ancient village

Bucknell is first mentioned in William the Conqueror's 'Great Description of England' of 1086, the Domesday Book, at which time it straddled the boundary between Shropshire and Herefordshire. It was not until boundary changes in 1555 that it came together in Shropshire. Back in 1086, the manor was held by Ranulph de Mortimer of Wigmore under a grant from Roger de Montgomery. Montgomery was one of William's principal barons and possibly one of his commanders in the field during the Battle of Hastings. William rewarded his faithful with lordship over land, in return for which they were expected to exert control over their subjects and thus subdue the country under the Norman rule. Created Earl of Shrewsbury and holding most of Shropshire and West Sussex as well as many manors elsewhere across the country, Roger de Montgomery was one of the richest and most powerful barons in the land. To carry out his bidding in Shropshire he divided the lands between Picot de Say of Stokesay and Ranulph. As a Marcher Lord, Ranulph established castles in his several manors close to the border, one of which overlooked a ford in the River Redlake from the north bank here at Bucknell. After William I's death, there was a power struggle for the throne, Ranulph (and indeed Robert) siding with the Duchy of Normandy against William Rufus, the Conqueror's son. But after the revolt failed, both cut their losses and made peace with the new king, thus holding on to their estates.

The village today

Dotted around the village are several old houses, one of the earliest being the 16th-century Old School House, which remained in use as such until the present school was built in 1865. A handful of others retain their thatch, and the village post office beside Tea in the Sticks retains an old-world feel. The River Redlake once powered several mills and when the railway

arrived in 1865, a coal depot and sawmill were established. But like most of Shropshire, the industrial age largely passed it by and Bucknell remains a peaceful backwater.

Dedicated to the Blessed Virgin Mary, Bucknell's church is believed to be a Norman foundation from around 1140, based on a document by the then Bishop of Coventry and Lichfield, Roger de Clinton, which refers to the establishment of several chapels in the Teme valley. The local lord, Andrew de Stainton subsequently gifted the church to Wigmore Abbey in return for sanctuary. He had offended his king, Henry II, and needed a place to hide until he could make arrangements to flee the country to Scotland. The church's oldest possession is the font, which is decorated with an interlaced cord motive that is suggestive of Saxon work. However it also bears a curious carving of a whiskered face, which some experts think is Norman. Other than that, little remains of its early fabric, it was largely rebuilt in the 14th century and then 'restored' in 1869 by the Victorians.

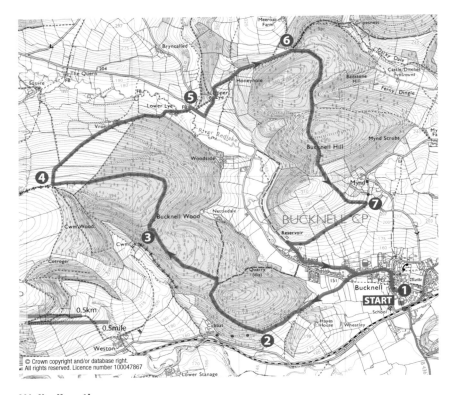

Walk directions

1 Walking north from the church, cross the river and swing left with the main lane, passing The Baron at Bucknell. At the next right-hand bend, keep ahead past a children's playground, shortly rising into trees. At a fork, keep right with the main lane, which later degrades to a track and in time reaches a junction.

2 Bear right to join another track from the right. Continue ahead, rising more steeply again through the forest. During the 19th century, timber became a major element in the local economy, with trees being felled and carted down to the timber yard by the station and used for all manner of purposes from building and fencing to furniture making. After 800m, watch for a track joining from the right. Immediately beyond, fork left on a lesser track rising at the edge of a felled area. At the top of the clearing, ignore a track off right and keep going, the ground beginning to fall away more steeply on the left.

3 Eventually meeting a junction of forest roads, go left and almost immediately swing right with the main track. Before long, the way bends left and the gradient eases. Later emerging from the trees, carry on across upland pasture for another 300m towards a gate.

4 Swing off right in front of it along a field track that falls in a long, gradual descent. Beyond the small farmhouse at Vron, the way continues as an old, hollow lane dropping through woodland. Reaching a junction in front of a gate, go right and then later bend left to a metalled track at Lower Lye. Follow it out right to a lane.

5 Be aware of traffic as you follow it right. After 100m, leave through a gate on the left and climb upfield beside the hedge. Ignore a field gate by the buildings at Roseheart Kingdom, going a little farther to a kissing gate. Through that turn right and continue to gain height, crossing a stile and passing Honeyhole Farm. Breaking into a field, maintain the steady plod up a green valley beside a plantation to emerge at the top onto a junction of forest roads at Hopton Wood.

6 Turn right past the small parking area and, ignoring a gate off left and track off right, keep ahead past a barrier. The rising track winds over the hill before falling in easy descent to a fork. Bear right (signed 'Short Loop') to a second junction and take the track ahead, marked as a byway. A final sharp pull takes you over the shoulder of Bucknell Hill, after which the track loses height steadily through the trees. Beyond a track off to 'Mynd Scrub', the way emerges from the forest. Carry on downhill for another 600m to a junction of signed tracks.

7 Take the one off sharp right, an initially hedged tack that gently descends across the slope of the hill. Eventually, drop out through a couple of gates by a cottage to continue along tarmac. At the bottom, bend sharp left by another cottage and follow the ongoing narrow lane. Meeting the main lane, go left past The Baron at Bucknell back into the village.

Walk 16 **Craven Arms and Stokesay Castle**

A nature reserve and picturesque castle with pleasant return beside the River Onny

What to expect:
Generally clear paths and tracks (after rain the way through Stoke Wood may occasionally be muddy); gradual ascents.

Distance/time: 7.2km/4½ miles. Allow 2 to 2½ hours
Start: Discovery Centre car park, Craven Arms
Grid ref: SO 435825
Ordnance Survey map: Explorer 217 (The Long Mynd & Wenlock Edge)
Refreshments: Cafés at Discovery Centre and Stokesay Castle
Transport: Bus and rail services to Craven Arms

Walk outline
Leaving the AONB's Discovery Centre at Craven Arms, the route circles out across the western fields, passing through the fringes of Sallow Coppice and Stoke Wood on its way to Stokesay Castle and the adjacent church. The return is above the eastern bank of the River Onny.

A 'new town' and medieval castle

Proudly dubbed the 'Gateway to the Marches', Craven Arms is a relatively new town, which only came into being during the 17th century. The earliest settlement in the area was established on the hilltop to the south east overlooking the valley across the River Onny. Dating back perhaps as early as the Bronze Age, Norton Camp is a large D-shaped enclosure, defended by deep double ditches and ramparts that extend over some seven hectares. It had three defended entrances and was blessed with a natural spring that rose nearby. Excavations have recovered pottery and other artefacts and revealed post-holes for several roundhouses, all suggesting that the camp was a sizeable, permanent settlement that probably remained occupied until the arrival of the Romans. However, despite its size, it is today rather unimpressive to the casual observer, the ramparts being much overgrown by trees while the central area has been under the plough since the 19th century.

The same cannot be said for nearby Stokesay Castle, which is perhaps one of the loveliest fortified manor houses you will come across. The manor was originally a Saxon settlement, but taken over after the Norman Conquest, when the lordship was given to one of William's knights, Picot

de Say, whose family later tagged their own name onto the original 'Stoc' which had simply meant 'place' or 'settlement'. By the 13th century the manor was held by Laurence of Ludlow, whose great wealth had derived from the Marches wool trade. By then, following Edward I's defeat of Llewelyn, peace was settling across the Marches and the need for stark, forbidding castle towers was becoming a thing of the past. In building his house, Laurence could now look to comfort and, as well as the obligatory great hall, he incorporated a solar with a magnificently decorated fireplace to which the family could retreat in relaxed privacy. But old habits died hard even then, and a licence to crenallate allowed him to add a battlemented tower and walls overlooking the moat. However, these were largely for show and the overhanging timber-framed upper storeys lend a distinctly fairytale look to the place. The timber-framed gatehouse was added in the 17th century, by which time the manor was held by the Cravens.

During the Civil War, Stokesay surrendered to the Parliamentarians, but the adjacent church suffered considerable damage when the Royalists later tried to retake the castle in 1646. The subsequent rebuilding of the church is one of few to have taken place during the Commonwealth period and inside, it is impressively furnished with a musicians' gallery, box pews and two canopied pews. Although partially slighted, the manor house remained largely intact as a home and was sympathetically restored in the 19th century. It formally opened its doors to the public in 1908 and later passed into the care of English Heritage.

The expansion of the turnpikes in the 17th century created a junction of roads just to the north of Stokesay, around which the 'Newtown' developed. To take advantage of the passing trade, the then Earl of Craven built a coaching inn, which was, not surprisingly, named after him. The town became a centre for the surrounding hamlets, with a stock market being opened to handle sales of sheep from the outlying farms. The arrival of the railway in 1852, with lines radiating in all directions brought another boost to the local economy. With there being more than one Newtown, the station was originally known as 'Craven Arms for Stokesay', but was eventually shortened simply to 'Craven Arms' and the town followed suit.

Here be giants

The area abounds in myth and legend and it is said that giants dwelt here, two brothers - one on Norton Camp and the other across the valley above Stoke Wood on View Edge. They kept their treasure in a strongbox hidden in the vaults of Stokesay Castle, sharing a key to the lock, which they tossed back and forth across the valley as and when each needed money. But, disaster struck when the key fell short into the castle's moat. Endless searching proved fruitless and there it still lies, as does the treasure beneath the castle, for the box is protected by a great raven, which will allow no one near unless they have the key!

The Shropshire Hills Discovery Centre

More recently Craven Arms has become the administrative centre for the Shropshire Hills AONB and is the site of the region's main information hub, the Shropshire Hills Discovery Centre. Roofed by living grass and set amidst 30 acres of riverside meadow and woodland it houses a fascinating exhibition that explores the shaping of the landscape and its history. One of the highlights is a full-size reconstruction of a mammoth's skeleton discovered at nearby Condover that dates from just after the last glacial period. There is also a realistic simulation of a balloon ride, which gives a fantastic aerial view of the beautiful Shropshire countryside.

Discovery Centre

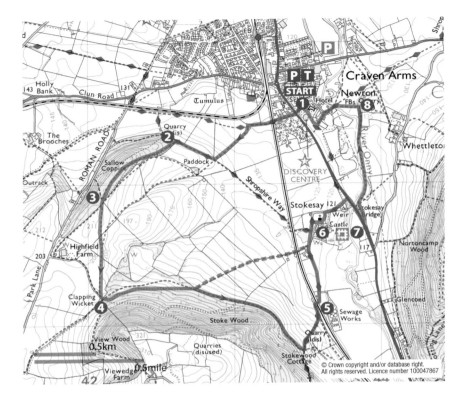

Walk directions

1 Leaving the Discovery Centre car park, walk to the main road. Cross to the footpath opposite and continue ahead along Dodds Lane. At the end, keep going between houses and beneath a railway track into a field. Head away by the left hedge to a stile in the corner and go right. At the top, pass through a gap and over another stile into Sallow Coppice.

2 To the left, the path initially remains by the edge of the wood before curving into the thick of the trees. Keep left at consecutive T-junctions, finally crossing a rickety stile back into open fields.

3 Go right into the adjacent field and strike out, aiming just right of the high point of the wooded hill ahead. Over a stile keep the same line across the ensuing fields to emerge at the corner onto the end of a track.

4 Turn left and immediately left again to follow the continuing track into Stoke Wood. After 400m, at a waypost, a path leaving left over fields is a shortcut to Stokesay Castle. Otherwise, continue ahead through the trees for another 800m, ultimately passing a barrier to a crossing track. Follow it down from the wood. Ignore a crossing track and instead, pass through the gate opposite and along a field track by the left hedge.

5 Emerging at the bottom, follow the ongoing track beside the railway. After winding over a level crossing (proceed with care) and then past a farm, the entrance to Stokesay Castle is on the right.

6 After exploring the castle, have a look at the church next door before winding around its eastern end to leave the churchyard onto a lane. Go right to the main road. Turn right again along the pavement, crossing a bridge over the River Onny.

7 After 100m, cross to a track and double back sharp left. It was the old road before the present bridge was built. Follow it to the end and go right down steps to a kissing gate. Bear left to a second gate and carry on along the riverbank. Farther on the path rises above a steep wooded bank to a kissing gate. Continue along a contained path and then keep beside a fence as it curves down the bank.

8 Walk on to a small footbridge and carry on across the corner of the next field to a fingerpost by the hedge, where there is a bridge across the river. On the far bank, follow a street away. Keep ahead past a junction and through a gate into the Discovery Centre park. Walk on past allotments and keep right to return to the centre.

Walk 17 **Titterstone Clee Hill**

Ramble over one of Shropshire's most intriguing hills

What to expect:

Short, initial stretch on vague path, otherwise the route is mostly clear; the ascent onto Titterstone, although long, is not unduly steep.

Distance/time: 6.4km/4 miles. Allow 2½ to 3 hours
Start: Car park by Titterstone Clee quarries
Grid ref: SO 593775
Ordnance Survey map: Explorer 203 (Ludlow)
Refreshments: The Hopton Crown at Hopton Wafers
Transport: None

Walk outline

Beginning beside abandoned quarry workings, the route returns briefly down the lane before turning off across open moor. Soon becoming indistinct, it falls steadily to Cleeton St Mary. After a short stretch of lane, the way returns to the moors, contouring the hill to Callowgate where it turns to tackle Titterstone Clee Hill from the north. It is a steady plod to the top, and after skirting above the western quarry workings, the path drops steeply beside an old incline back to the car park.

Titterstone Clee Hill

At 533m, Titterstone Clee Hill is Shropshire's third highest summit. It is one of the very few hills specifically identified on the 13th-century Mappa Mundi, the largest surviving map of the medieval known world, which is displayed in Hereford Cathedral. The hill has been a noted landmark for millennia; Bronze Age people constructed a burial cairn on its summit and some 2,000 years later, an Iron Age community raised a defensive enclosure, its ramparts stoutly fortified from the blocks of ice-shattered stone that litter the hilltop. The 4,000 year-old cairn lies just east of the trig column, but part of the Iron Age defensive walls have been lost to the massive quarries that subsequently ate into the upper hill.

On a clear day the view is perhaps one of the best in England, panning from the Brecon Beacons across to Cadair Idris, Shining Tor in the Peak District and the Cotswolds. Today, its strategic location is exploited by radar arrays, the largest of which control air traffic routes across the Midlands, whilst the smaller is used by the Met Office to monitor cloud and precipitation across central England and Wales.

Geologists will tell you that the fractured outcrops and rock debris around the summit are a product of the last glaciation, but local legend gives a

different story. The massive rocks by the summit are known as the Giant's Chair, from which the incumbent giant looked across to his neighbours on Abdon Burf and Brown Clee. These fractious giants whiled away their time hurling rocks at each other! Reputedly, the exertion eventually exhausted them to the point of collapse and the local folk took advantage of the lull to bury them. An annual wake used to be held on the hill to keep them away, but the practice has died out – so beware! Watch out too for a spectral hound with glowing eyes and a jewel-encrusted collar. But its bark is worse than its bite, for the beast will skulk off if challenged.

From the early medieval period, coal, ironstone and copper were mined, initially from adits and clusters of shallow bell pits and then later, deep mines. Many of the surrounding villages grew specifically to accommodate the workers. The quarries were opened during the 19th century, exploiting an igneous intrusion of dhustone (Welsh meaning blackstone). It is a hard dolerite, which was used for road surfacing and the production of setts and also as building stone for the construction of the docks at Cardiff. Although Clee Hill quarry still operates, those on Titterstone Clee ceased working in the 1930s and the area around the car park, even on the brightest of days, has an air of dereliction and abandonment. The massive quarry faces and long inclines from the summit down to the railway at Bitterley still emphasise the scale of the operation.

Cleeton St Mary

The original settlement was established high up on marginal farmland around a moated manor house. But depopulation during the Black Death and a change of climate prompted migration down the hill. Coal and ironstone mining, and later quarrying, helped supplement meagre incomes from farming.

Back in the USSR

At the southern foot of the hill, the village of Cleehill once boasted Shropshire's highest pub. Originally called the Craven Arms, it became known as The Kremlin during the 1980s, because Radio Moscow could sometimes be heard playing from the silent jukebox. With no intervening high ground as far as the Ural Mountains, errant signals were apparently bouncing off Titterstone's radar masts!

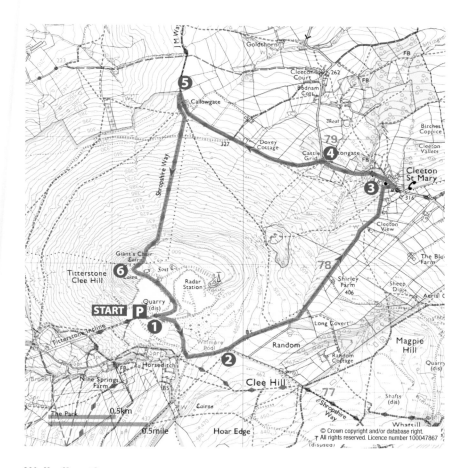

© Crown copyright and/or database right.
All rights reserved. Licence number 100047867

Walk directions

1 From the parking area, walk back down the lane for 400m. Immediately after crossing a stream and before reaching a wooden fingerpost, leave left on a faint trod across the moor above the shallow groove of the stream. Rising towards a saddle it crests the rise by the corner of a fence.

2 Carry on with the fence to your right. Passing a waypost, keep ahead as the fence moves away and ignore a crossing track, a little farther on. The way continues in gentle descent at the edge of the moor, ultimately meeting the end of a track by the church at Cleeton St Mary.

3 Turn right past the front of the church, swinging around the eastern end of the church yard to double back below it along the main lane. After dipping to cross Shirley Brook, the lane eventually rises to a bend.

4 Leave just before a cattle grid, turning off left on a rough path. Following a gentle climb beside the right boundary, it levels off across the hillside. After almost 1.2km approaching the farm at Callowgate, the path curves right. At that point, leave the fence and walk ahead to a waymark.

5 Turn left and (ignoring a more distinct path bearing right) follow the path rising ahead towards the 'golf ball' perched on top of Titterstone Clee Hill. Farther on, the way broadens and climbs more steeply before later easing again. Watch for the path then raking off to the right above a slope of broken rock to lessen the steepness of the final pull. Shortly gaining the summit plateau, walk on to the trig column that appears ahead at the western end of the hill.

6 The way back is sharp left, passing right of a low building. Following 'Shropshire Way' marker posts, bear right off the cinder access track to pick up a green path that runs out along a tongue of high ground, which separates the two main quarry workings. Towards the far end, the path swings right down the groove of an incline to meet a track at the bottom. Go right to a hairpin bend and the car park.

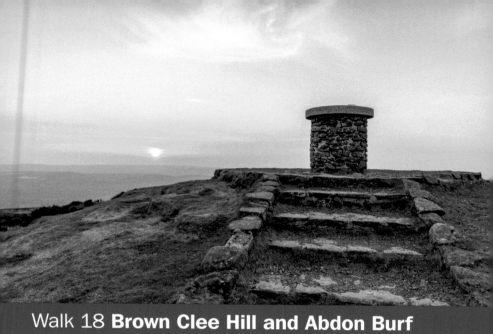

Walk 18 **Brown Clee Hill and Abdon Burf**

Climb to the highest point in Shropshire for a view extending over 14 counties

What to expect:

Generally good paths and tracks; only a couple of steeper climbs

Distance/time: 9.7km/6 miles. Allow 3 to 3½ hours
Start: Brown Clee picnic area
Grid ref: SO 607872
Ordnance Survey map: Explorer 217 (The Long Mynd & Wenlock Edge)
Refreshments: The Boyne Arms at nearby Burwarton
Transport: Bus service through nearby Burwarton

Walk outline

Beginning from a small picnic area beside a minor lane south of Ditton Priors, the walk rises through conifer plantations to the upper hill. After winding past old workings to the summit, there is a gentle descent across open moor back to the trees. The final stretch is along a quiet lane.

The Clee Hill range

The Clee Hills run almost north-south for some 24km/15 miles, defining the eastern edge of the Shropshire Hills. To the south is Titterstone Clee (Walk 17), while here Abdon Burf and Clee Burf form the twin tops of Brown Clee Hill. At 540m Abdon Burf, marks the county's highest point and on a clear day offers a superb view over the surrounding countryside. Shropshire's other hills stride out to the west: Wenlock Edge, The Long Mynd and the Stiperstones, with Plynlimon and Cadair Idris a distant backdrop. To the south rise the Malvern and Cotswold hills, while to the east are the Clent Hills and towns of the West Midlands. Farther north is Cannock Chase, the Peak District and Winter Hill on the edge of the far-off Pennines. In all, it is claimed that the panorama extends across 14 counties.

Iron Age farmers could not ignore such a commanding position and, during the 1st millennium BC, established a large settlement on the summit of Abdon Burf, one of three in the immediate area. A survey in the middle of the 19th century identified a single ditch and rampart enclosing around 30 acres, in which over forty stone circles, the foundations of living or storage huts, were laid out in parallel rows. The site has since been lost to quarrying, as has that on Clee Burf to the south, but the third survives on Nordy Bank over to the west and remains an impressive sight.

The summits of the Clee Hills share a similar geology and all three tops have been extensively mined and quarried since the early medieval period.

Their coal seams are said to be the highest in Britain and lie in proximity to both iron and copper ores as well as limestone. Mining was undertaken from small bell pits whose collapsed shafts and spoil heaps litter the tops of the hills, with the ore being processed at ironworks over in Corve Dale. The advent of motor transport created a demand for stone to surface the country's rapidly expanding road network and the hard dolerite (here called dhustone) outcropping on the Clee summits was ideal for the purpose. The desolation of flooded pits, mounds of waste and ruined buildings scattered across the hilltop give scale to the size of the undertaking. The largest range of buildings are the remains of a crushing plant and hoppers, from which the stone was loaded into wagons and winched down the hill on a steep inclined tramway to the railhead at Ditton Priors, where there were concrete and tarmac plants. After the quarries closed in 1936, many of the former quarrymen found employment in an extensive Royal Navy ammunition depot, which was established at the edge of Ditton Priors.

In their heyday, the quarries were the largest source of employment in the area, drawing men from as far away as Ludlow. Some, however, wanting to live closer to their work, established themselves as squatters on the common land and built cottages on the hillside. Previously, the area had been used by local people as common grazing, with the upper hill being divided between the surrounding hamlets. With the closure of the quarries, many of the cottages were abandoned and their remains can still be found across the moor. A handful, however, were maintained as housing for workers on the Burwarton Estate.

Remains of quarry buildings on Abdon Burf

A stately home

Burwarton Hall stands just outside the village at the foot of the hill (not
open to the public). Owned by the Holland family since the 15th century,
the estate passed to the Viscounts Boyne (who originally came from
Scotland, but also held lands in Ireland) by marriage in the 18th century.
The present house was built in the Italianate style during the 1830s and
is surrounded by formal gardens and a landscaped park. But although
successively extended until the 1920s, it was partly demolished after the
Second World War to provide a more manageable house, which remains
the family seat.

Although Brown Clee's summit is hardly pretty, the pleasant ramble up
and down is more than compensation. The scattered industrial heritage
provides an interesting dimension, while a topograph helps place the hill in
the context of its surroundings. Across the moor, vestiges of old wildflower
meadow and wet flushes attract butterflies and dragonflies, while in the
skies, watch for skylark, curlew, peregrine and barn owls. Look out too for a
memorial near The Five Springs (Point (6)), which remembers 23 Allied and
German airmen who died as a result of plane crashes on the hill during the
Second World War.

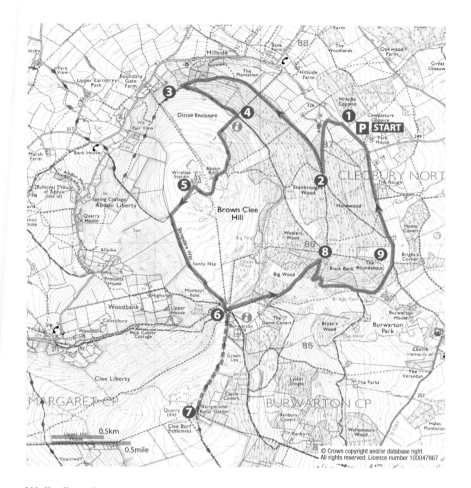

Walk directions

1 There are several places to park beside the lane. Leave through a gate by the picnic area sign from which a marked path climbs to the right up through bracken. After curving left, keep with the higher path, rising at the edge of the woodland and eventually meeting a forest road.

2 Follow it sharp right, passing through a gate to run below the plantation. Ignore a crossing tarmac track rising steeply up the hill and continue with the ongoing track opposite, which eventually ends at a gate.

3 Through that go left, above the trees, shortly meeting the tarmac track you encountered earlier, which follows the course of an old tramway incline.

4 Turn right up the hill towards hillocks of quarry spoil. Swinging left, carry on past the ruined buildings and relics of abandoned workings. Approaching the masts that dominate the top of the hilltop, leave the metalled track for a gravel path on the left and climb steps to the summit topograph.

5 Descend the steps and turn right on a clear path heading south west across the hillside. After 400m, approaching a gate, go left by a waymark and follow the fence away. Continue beyond its corner towards the saddle between Abdon Burf and its lesser satellite to the south, where a seat above The Five Springs looks down the valley to Cockshutford.

6 If not pressed for time, carry on along the broad spine to the second summit of Clee Burf (Point 7). Otherwise, leave the main path left to a gate and pass through a belt of trees. Keep going at the edge of woodland, passing through another gate and eventually joining a track from the right.

8 Some 550m later, approaching a gate near a lodge hidden in the trees, double back right on a grass path that winds down across the open woodland of the park. Shortly meeting another track, go left, passing through a gate onto the bend of a metalled track. Follow it ahead.

9 Farther on, bear left as another track joins and continue through the park, eventually leaving onto the corner of a lane. Follow it ahead back to the picnic area.

Walk 19 **Wenlock Edge**

Explore the narrow ridge of Wenlock Edge and rolling farmland below its northern slopes

What to expect:
Woodland and field tracks, occasional indistinct trods; one sustained climb

Distance/time: 10.5km/6½ miles. Allow 3 to 3½ hours
Start: National Trust woodland car park beside B4371 at Presthope
Grid ref: SO 583975
Ordnance Survey map: Explorer 241 (Shrewsbury)
Transport: None

Walk outline
From a small National Trust car park beside the ridgeway road, the route drops through woodland on the northern flank before climbing back to pick up the trackbed of the old Wellington to Craven Arms Railway. Farther along, it drops off the ridge to the hamlet of Hughley and follows the valley of Hughley upstream. The final stage heads back onto Wenlock Edge, ascending steeply, for a fine stretch along the crest above extensive abandoned quarries and past an impressive bank of limekilns.

A history of quarrying

Running for over 25km/16 miles, the narrow Wenlock Edge escarpment is the remnant of an ancient coral reef formed in a shallow tropical sea. One of the richest such sources of coral, trilobite, crinoid and shell fossils in the country, its limestone has been quarried from the medieval period. The stone for Much Wenlock Priory and Buildwas Abbey was cut here and later, the fledgling ironworks in Coalbrookdale used the limestone as a flux for smelting ore, a use which escalated towards the end of the 18th century as the Industrial Revolution got underway.

Although some quarrying continues today towards the northern end of the ridge, the main workings have now been closed and it is hoped that they will be returned to nature as a reserve. The thick woodland, open grassland and abandoned quarry floors below the escarpment are rich in plant life and over 40 separate species have been identified in just a single square metre. Wander through as spring segues into summer and you will find bluebells and wild garlic aplenty as well as primrose, yellow archangel, dog violet, marsh marigold and lesser celandine, not to mention orchids, which thrive on thin soils. Parts of the wood have been managed for centuries, the trees coppiced to produce charcoal. Hazel, ash, limes and wych elm are amongst those to look out for, the hazel providing fruit for mammals such as the tiny dormice, which, in turn, are food for owls. Other birds to be seen include nuthatch, woodcock and buzzard.

A prodigious leap

The high viewpoint passed above the quarries is known as Major's Leap, taking its name from Major Thomas Smallman of nearby Wilderhope Manor. He sided with the King during the Civil War, but Cromwell's forces descended on the manor and he was taken prisoner. Although managing to escape he was pursued on horseback along Wenlock Edge and in a last-ditch attempt to avoid recapture, he leapt over the cliff. Miraculously Smallman managed to get away, but his horse was killed and its ghostly form has been seen along the hill ever since.

Birth and death of a railway

Part of the walk follows the course of the former Wellington to Craven Arms Railway. Begun from Wellington in 1857, it worked its way along the ridge, reaching Presthope by the end of 1864. It took stone and lime from the quarries to the industry of Coalbrookdale and beyond, bringing back coal for the limekilns. After a tunnel was cut through the ridge at Presthope, the line was eventually completed to Craven Arms in 1867, providing the Great Western Railway with a link from Manchester to the West Country and South Wales. However, the route never realised its full potential due to steep gradients and being a single line. The line was finally closed in 1963.

History in the rocks

At the end of the walk, the route passes through the former Knowle Quarry. The old working face reveals a cross section through the reef, illustrating how the conditions of its formation changed over time. Clear waters allowed coral to thrive, but there were also periods when silt and clay washed in and smothered its growth. The quarry fed limestone to the nearby bank of kilns, which produced a continuous supply of lime both for the ironworks and spreading on fields as a fertiliser. They were built during the second half of the 19th century and remained in use until 1925.

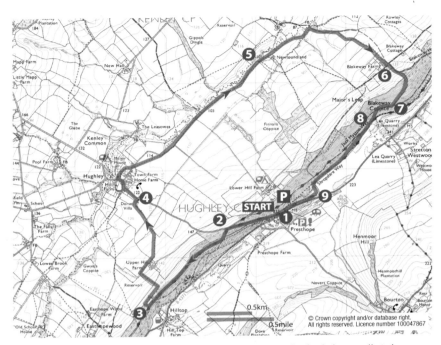

1 Follow a track through a gate behind the car park. As it immediately bends, leave left along a path to Easthopewood, which falls sharply through the trees. Meeting a wide farm-track at the bottom, follow it left to a lane.

2 Cross to the 'Shropshire Way' opposite, which climbs to a crossing track - the old railway. To the left is the now-gated portal of a short tunnel, but the onward route is to the right. After 1.2km, and 200 metres beyond a path up to Ippikin's Rock, watch for a crossing path.

3 Follow it right, soon crossing a stile into a meadow. Head on, swinging right halfway down to contour the slope. Eventually reaching a lone tree, drop left to a stile in the hedge. Head out to a second stile and across a narrower strip to a small gate. Go through and turn right beside the hedge past Upper Hill Farm, continuing beyond its end to a waymarked stile in the short hedge ahead. Over that, strike out half-left to a small gate-gap halfway along the bottom hedge. Through that, turn right, curving within the corner beside the hedge. Approaching Dorset Villa, leave the field and follow a track out to a lane.

4 Go left through Hughley. Approaching the church, take a track off right. After a few metres, abandon it for a narrow footpath on the right and continue at the edge of conifers to emerge in a small field. Bear right to a stile beside a gate onto a farm lane. Cross to a stile almost opposite and strike half-left left across a small paddock. Over consecutive stiles, cross a track and maintain the line across a field to a gate at an indented corner. Rejoining the lane, follow it on for 1.6km.

5 Beyond the second cattle grid, fork left, briefly following a field track. As that then curves downhill, bear right past the hedge of Newfoundland and continue along a meadow above the wooded course of Hughley Brook. After 400m, towards the far end, drop right to find a stile into trees. Cross a shallow stream and walk left along the foot of a rough field. Ignoring a footbridge, carry on above the stream for another 350m before breaking into the corner of more open grazing. Bear right beside an old wooded boundary. Through a gate at the top, continue at the edge of a crop field to emerge onto a track by Blakeway Farm.

6 Go left and immediately right up a broad path into woodland. Emerging into a clearing, stick with the main track, which swings right to resume the steep climb.

7 Meeting a broad track at the top go right towards Presthope. Shortly, bear left at a fork. Another stiff pull leads to a ridge-top path above the abandoned Lea Quarry. Go right, shortly reaching Major's Leap, a rocky platform offering a spectacular prospect Shropshire's countryside.

8 Carry on for another 800m before entering trees. Where the path splits, take the left branch signed 'Bird Hide' and 'Limekilns'. Dropping past a path off left, which leads to the old powder store, it shortly reaches a junction by railings above old limekilns.

9 The path left drops to the working floor below, while the way back is to the right, winding past a bird hide and the former Knowle Quarry. Continue up steps to a junction and go left back to the car park.

Walk 20 **The Wrekin**

A strenuous walk over one of Shropshire's iconic Hills

What to expect:
Generally good hill paths and tracks; steep ascent and descent of The Wrekin

Distance/time: 11.3km/7 miles. Allow 4 to 4½ hours
Start: Car park below quarries at Lawrence's Hill on minor lane north of Little Wenlock
Grid ref: SJ 638092
Ordnance Survey map: Explorer 242 (Telford, Ironbridge & The Wrekin)
Refreshments: The Halfway House Café or the Huntsman, Little Wenlock
Transport: None

Walk outline
Beginning from a low col breaking the Wrekin ridge, the route strikes for the walk's highpoint. It is a strenuous pull and an even steeper descent (take care when wet or icy), but is followed with a gentle contour around the hill's wooded eastern flank. The route winds on past Wenlock's Wood and around Maddock's Hill to fall through Limekiln Wood. The final leg is through the lush woods of The Ercall, passing abandoned quarries that reveal some of the hill's complex geology.

Volcanic, but not a volcano

Believe the geologists and they'll tell you that The Wrekin was created from layers of volcanic rock and ash that emanated from a nearby volcano some 560 million years ago. The evidence can be seen in the abandoned quarries on The Ercall, passed towards the end of the walk, where you can see the ancient, hard volcanic rocks exposed, side by side with strata of sedimentary sandstones that were laid down when the region was subsequently washed by the fringes of an ancient tropical sea. And even the ripples produced by waves lapping on the sandy shore have been preserved in the flat slabs of stone.

However, folklore has a more colourful explanation and concerns a testy Welsh giant, who had a beef with the good people of Shrewsbury. Determined to remove the thorn in his side, he dug out a huge spadeful of Welsh earth and set off to dam the River Severn and thus flood the town. But lost and tired near Wellington (Telford wasn't around in those days) he stopped a cobbler on his way home and, explaining his mission, asked the way. The quick-thinking cobbler, not wishing to see his profitable customers washed away, tipped out the sackful of shoes he was carrying home to mend and said "You've still a mighty long way to go, just look at all these shoes I've worn out coming from there'. Thoroughly demoralised the giant sighed and uptipped his spade where he stood and then scraped the mud off his shoes before turning back towards home. You've guessed - the two piles of spoil he left behind were The Wrekin and The Ercall.

Whatever its origins, The Wrekin is an impressive hill commanding an expansive view to the main body of the Shropshire Hills. However, despite many assertions to the contrary, Snowdon cannot be seen from the top, it is not that it is too far away (110km/70 miles), but just that the Berwyn range is in the way. Nevertheless, it is reckoned that 15 separate counties are visible and the hill was the inspiration for Tolkien's Middle Earth in The Lord of the Rings. Today, the top is dominated by television and communication transmitters, but 2,000 years ago the hill was the tribal capital for the Cornovii, whose territory covered all of present-day Shropshire and extended across Cheshire to the Wirral peninsula.

An ancient stronghold

Commanding the high ground above marsh woodland and the floodplain of the River Severn, the settlement probably dates back to the Bronze Age, but around 500BC was augmented by a complex defence of ramparts and ditches extending over more than 0.75km of the highest part of the ridge. The intricate entrances at Hell Gate and Heaven Gate can still be seen, where the embankments turn back on themselves and were additionally fortified by stone-built strongholds. Inside the defences, traces have been found of numerous hut platforms and it is reckoned that up to 1,000 people lived here.

Despite the seemingly unassailable position, it was no defence against the Romans when they arrived around AD47. Two Roman spear heads were found on the hilltop and archaeological evidence suggests that the huts were burnt to the ground. The settlement was abandoned and instead the Romans established a camp about 8km/5 miles away by the River Severn, Viroconium (present day Wroxeter). It was only occupied by the military for a relatively short time but by the year AD88 had developed as a thriving civilian settlement, at one stage having a population of around 15,000 and considered the fourth largest town in Roman Britain. It continued in use for a while after the Romans left at the beginning of the 5th century, but it too was eventually abandoned, and over the years its walls were quarried for ready-cut building stone. Although only partly excavated, it remains an impressive sight, the 'Old Work' being the largest free-standing Roman structure in the country, with an extensive bathhouse nearby. An authentic Roman town house has been reconstructed on the site and houses an interesting exhibition that vividly illustrates life at the time. The site is well worth visiting after the walk.

Former industry

Beyond the hill, the walk meanders through rolling woodland, itself steeped in history. During the Saxon and early Norman period, the area was part of an extensive royal hunting forest and parts of the wood may be remnants of wild wood that were not subsequently cleared for cultivation and husbandry. Nevertheless, the patches of woodland that remained have been managed for centuries, trees selectively felled for timber with others being coppiced to produce a regular supply of small wood for charcoal burning, wattle making and turning. Hidden amongst the trees are mounds and hollows associated with coal mining, which was undertaken from bell pits, and part of the walk runs along the causeway of an old tramline that ran through the wood to Steeraway. Levelled floors and low outcrops betray small stone quarries while nearby are ruins of kilns where limestone was burned to make lime for mortar, fertiliser or ironmaking. Returning over The Ercall the route passes larger quarries were hard dolerite was extracted for roadmaking, some of which was used in the construction of the M54. The abundance and variety of wildflowers is an indicator of the age of a wood, bluebells in particular thriving in ground that has long been undisturbed. Look out for butterflies such as green hairstreak and dingy skipper, and you might also hear a woodpecker too.

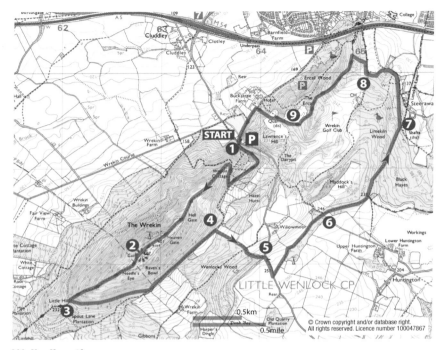

Walk directions

1 Leaving the car park, go right and then fork left. Almost immediately, turn sharp left up a broad track onto The Wrekin. Climb around a bend to a junction and there keep right, the gradient shortly easing past the Halfway House and Café. At the next junction, swing left up the spine of the hill, the ascent soon steepening through the outer ramparts of the fort at Hell Gate. Continue upwards, passing through further ramparts at Heaven Gate and on to the top.

2 The ongoing ridge path descends past more outcrops before dramatically steepening into trees, this section demanding care, especially in wet or icy conditions. The path eventually drops to a small saddle, marked by a broad crossing track. The way ahead rises onto Little Hill, the final outpost of the ridge. But, as trees obscure the view, the detour is hardly worth the effort.

3 Instead, turn left along the broad track, which undulates back around the southern slopes of The Wrekin. Bear left as another track later joins and continue within the fringe of the wood for another 800m.

4 Look for a waypost marking a path off right out of the wood. Over a stile, head away beside Wenlocks Wood to meet a farm track, continuing along a path opposite, now within the trees, to reach a lane.

5 Follow it to the top of the hill and leave through a gate on the left along a field track. Where it bends, keep ahead through a kissing gate, maintaining the line to the corner of woodland opposite. The onward path adopts the course of an old tramway through thick scrub, eventually passing a track off right and reaching a crossing track.

6 Keep ahead through a cycle barrier and continue with the main path as it descends through Limekiln Wood.

7 At another barrier, the path splits. Fork left and carry on past old workings and sunken kilns. Carry on as it joins a lower path, keeping right and then ahead with red waymarks at successive junctions. Wind between dark pools and past a redundant kissing gate to a fork. Bear left up steps and then down to a junction. Go right, leaving the wood by the entrance to the Wrekin Golf Club.

8 Follow the drive downhill for some 70m then leave through a gap on the left, signed 'Wrekin Forest Trails'. Over a stream, swing left and climb to a crossing path. Turn left, still following red markers. Eventually rising to a T-junction, go left again, the way now losing height and leading to a fork. Keep left with the lower path, dropping to a clearing below The Ercall quarry.

9 Walk ahead past a pool and then more quarries before meeting a lane by Buckatree Hall Hotel. The way back lies to the left, though some lane can be avoided on a parallel path leaving immediately before the exit barrier.

Useful Information

Please follow the **Country Code** at all times.

Respect – Protect – Enjoy

www.gov.uk/countryside-code

Shropshire Hills AONB Partnership

The Shropshire Hills AONB website has information on things to see and do, plus a host of practical details to help plan your visit.

www.shropshirehillsaonb.co.uk

Visit Shropshire

Shropshire's official tourism website covers everything from accommodation and special events to attractions and adventure. www.shropshiretourism.co.uk

Shropshire Tourist Information Centres

These provide free information on everything from accommodation and transport to what's on and walking advice.

Bishop's Castle - 01588 630023 - info@bishopscastletownhall.co.uk

Bridgnorth - 01746 763358 - bridgnorth.library@shropshire.gov.uk

Church Stretton - 01694 723133 - churchstretton.library@shropshire.gov.uk

Craven Arms, Shropshire Hills Discovery Centre - 01588 676060 - info@shropshirehillsdiscoverycentre.co.uk

Ludlow – 01584 875053 visitors@ludlowassemblyrooms.co.uk

Market Drayton - 01630 652105 - marketdrayton.library@shropshire.gov.uk

Much Wenlock - 01952 727679 - shropshiremuseums@shropshire.gov.uk

Shrewsbury, Museum and Gallery - 01743 258888 - visitorinfo@shropshire.gov.uk

Shropshire Hills Shuttles

Services run at weekends and Bank Holidays through the summer season
01743 254740 - www.shropshirehillsshuttles.co.uk

For other bus services - Traveline - 0345 303 6760 - www.travelinemidlands.co.uk

Rail

Main line rail services radiate across the country from Shrewsbury, passing through the Shropshire Hills AONB to Ludlow and Knighton - www.nationalrail.co.uk